GW00746052

·WHITICISMS·

Mike Whitney

with cartoons by Scott Rigney

IRONBARK
Pan Macmillan Australia

First published 1995 in Ironbark by Pan Macmillan Australia Pty Limited
St Martins Tower, 31 Market Street, Sydney

Copyright © Mike Whitney and Geoff Armstrong 1995

All rights reserved. No part of this book may be reproduced or
transmitted in any form or by any means, electronic or
mechanical, including photocopying, recording or by any
information storage and retrieval system, without prior
permission in writing from the publisher.

National Library of Australia
cataloguing-in-publication data:

Whitney, Mike, 1959– .
Whiticisms.

ISBN 0 330 35624 0.

1. Whitney, Mike, 1959– . 2. Cricket players -
Australia - Biography. I. Title.

796.358092
Typeset in Sabon 11/14pt by DOCUPRO, Sydney
Printed in Australia by Australian Print Group

To all the clubs, companies and conferences;
to everyone who's listened to my stories and laughed.
Many thanks! It was my pleasure!

Acknowledgements

Many thanks to Geoff Armstrong for his persistence and dedication to this project. A true pro! Also, to Pan Macmillan, for taking on my second book. Thanks Deb! And finally, to all my team-mates, who have given me many hours of laughter — and headaches — through those 'golden years'.

Contents

A Stand-Up Mike

The first time I ever stood up on stage and spoke at a function was at a Cricket Society meeting in Adelaide. Now, the cricket society guys are genuine lovers of the game, but compared to most they are a fairly sedate audience. I have a lot of great friends involved in the Cricket Society there, and I'm sure they wouldn't mind me saying they are not a flamboyant group.

They are in many ways the perfect audience for an inexperienced cricketer about to begin his or her speaking career. As well as being fairly discerning, they are also so passionate about the game they would find absolutely anything remotely connected with cricket extremely interesting. They are also a very orderly and polite crowd; not the sort of people to jump up and hurl abuse, or beer glasses, if you weren't any good. However, when I was called up to make a brief address on that day I was close to terrified.

It was late 1981. I had just come back from England after my incredible call-up into the Australian team. NSW were playing South Australia in Adelaide at the time of the Society dinner, and it was a tradition for at least a couple of the visiting players to be invited to the function. Geoff Lawson was invited as the guest speaker, and I was asked if I'd like to come along as well. As a non-speaking guest.

Henry entertained the lads and ladies with the story of his experiences on the tour of England and how he was recovering from his back injury. It all seemed to be received extremely well. He finished to polite applause and then the MC stood up and said: 'Wasn't that a fantastic address by the NSW and Australian fast bowler, Geoff Lawson? We are all delighted to see he's recovered from his injury.'

Then he continued: 'As you all know, that injury is the reason Michael Whitney gained a place in the Australian Test team in England. And, ladies and gentleman, I'm sure you'd all like to hear a few words from Michael.'

I immediately thought: 'He's kidding! What am I going to say? I've never spoken in public before.'

But everyone was clapping. I stumbled up on stage and whispered to this bloke: 'Mate, I've played 10 first-class games. What the hell do you want me to talk about?'

'Why don't you just tell us all about how you were selected to play for Australia,' he suggested.

And then he handed me the mike, which seemed to be shaking an awful lot.

'Ah . . . well . . . Good evening, ladies and gentleman. Ummm, well, it's very nice to be here. Ah . . . As some of you might know, I went over to England at the end of last season to play for Fleetwood . . .'

Forty minutes later I had told the whole story — of going to league cricket in the north of England, of playing for Gloucestershire with Zaheer Abbas, Mushtaq Mohammad and Mike Procter, and then being selected for Australia. Of rooming with DK Lillee and playing in the final two Ashes Tests, of knocking David Gower over for my first Test wicket and on and on and on.

Fortunately they loved it. So much so that one of the people there actually had excerpts from the speech published in the next edition of the Cricket Society quarterly journal. All I had done, once the initial nerves had disappeared, was be myself. It seemed as if the words had been rolling off the tongue without me really even thinking about it — and this nearly had me in a bit of trouble. At one point I was relating how I had first signed up with my league club, Fleetwood.

'I went to Fleetwood, which is north of Blackpool,' I explained. 'Now, Fleetwood is a fishing village and when the trawlers came in, if the wind was blowing the wrong way, it used to remind me of a girl I knew at Maroubra . . .'

The sober mouths of the members of the Cricket Society all dropped at once. 'No! No! You don't understand,' I pleaded. 'Her father owned a fish shop!'

I hadn't realised what I'd said. The Fleetwood breeze really did remind me of that ex-girlfriend's father's fish shop (I can recall thinking exactly that on one of my first days in England), but when I looked back on my speech later, I wished I'd never said it. Mind you, I still use the line from time to time.

From that unlikely introduction to public speaking I graduated to what I like to call the 'country circuit'. In fact, I was speaking at a number of city gigs as well, but the ones I remember most vividly are the trips to the country. In those days, the perfect scenario was a combination of three functions over a weekend, with $250 to be collected after each of them. That sort of money, at that time in my life, was a bundle.

One such trifecta occurred over a weekend in the Hunter Valley of NSW, when I spoke at functions on successive nights at Cessnock, then Maitland and finally Dungog. I drove up with my then girlfriend, now wife, Debbie, in our fragile, old '68 Holden Torana, did gigs on the Friday night, Saturday night and Sunday night, and came home with $750 in my kick, thinking: 'What a HUGE weekend!'

The talk I did at Dungog remains one of the more interesting of my life. Dungog is, of course, the birthplace of Doug Walters. What more can you say? I'm not 100 per cent sure, but I think

it was a presentation night of some kind. What I can definitely recall is that the people who invited me there were very friendly, and that on the wall of the hall where the function was being held was the 'Doug Walters Honour Roll', which listed the names of a number of local sporting champions. I genuinely felt privileged just to be in the room and in the town, let alone speaking at their function.

There must have been 150 people in the hall when I spoke. And only one waitress. She was a tiny lady, in an ultra-conservative blue dress that was covered by a plain white apron, and must have been about 60 years old. When she brought the entree out she brought them out two at a time, so the serving of meals was a drawn-out process. I was due to do my bit after the main meal, which meant I wasn't on until a little bit later than usual. But, what the heck, this was a country gig, the pace of the place was that little bit slower than city living, and the locals didn't mind if things only chugged along, so long as they had a beer in hand and a friendly face alongside.

As soon as the roast chicken with vegies was finished I was introduced, and before long I was right into it. But then, about 15 minutes in, I was distracted by the vision, out of the corner of my eye, of the large door of the kitchen swinging open, and the elderly waitress starting to walk straight towards me. My first reaction was — no trouble, she's going to walk behind me to gather a couple more empty plates. But then, when she came up next to me, she stopped. I turned, not knowing what to say or do. Then I quietly asked: 'Yes?'

She leaned forward, stood as high as she could, I leaned down towards her, and she whispered: 'The chef said to tell you the ice cream is melting.'

And then she turned and walked back to the kitchen.

I was gone completely. I fumbled about for a couple of minutes but my presentation was over . . . killed off.

I'll always remember that night in Dungog as just about the hardest $250 I ever made.

Since those days, I have moved slowly up the public speaking ladder, to a point where I can more or less pick the functions I want to do. And the variety of people who want me at their gigs has also broadened, so that today I'm involved in business seminars and conferences as well as sporting functions. Obviously, a gig is only as good as the people you are talking to but the truth is, I love them all.

It's not something that I set out to do, but it is now a significant part of how I make my living. I never meant it to be like this, even though my family have always been outrageous story tellers. Whenever we get together, we start reminiscing. Debbie will say: 'Not those stories . . . AGAIN!' But away we go, and always the yarns are embellished with accents and often they can become very animated as well.

Sometimes my presentations for clubs or businesses are required to be funny, sometimes motivational, sometimes both. As far as motivation goes, I can only tell people how M. Whitney has achieved what he has achieved. That might not strike a chord with anyone in the audience at all, but if at least a few can gain something positive from just one point I have emphasised, then I believe that me being there has been a success.

I never thought I was the world's greatest bowler. Far from it. But I had a few things on my side. I was motivated, I was dedicated, and I was a great trainer. And I wanted more than anything to be out there. There was not one day in my career, ever, whether I was playing for Australia, Randwick, NSW, Fleetwood, Gloucestershire, Haslingden or whoever, when I didn't want to lace my boots up. There were times when I was sore, and I'd say to myself, 'I can't get out there,' but I'd always give myself a gee-up: 'You've *got* to get out there, c'mon.' And out I'd go. I always thought that if I gave some other guy an opportunity he was going to take my spot.

The thing about most people who set out to attempt something is that they are never really ready for that step. There's one thing I always said to myself before I went on the cricket field. Are you ready? Are you physically ready, and mentally ready? Do you have your kneeguard? Are the shoelaces in your boot right? Because the last thing I wanted to happen was for me to be on fire, but then break a shoelace and give the batsmen a couple of minutes respite. If you have a dodgy shoelace or a spike missing from your boot, then you're not ready.

That sort of thing to me is lousy preparation. Preparation is the key. If you're prepared better than your opponent then many more times than not you're going to win.

I reckon you can draw a lot of parallels between sport and business. To be a success in professional sport requires many of the same qualities that are needed to succeed in business. You need ability, sure, but you also need ambition, persistence and a little bit of courage. And you also need a lot of great people around you, as I had during my cricketing life. I had a great chiropractor, brilliant physiotherapists, magnificent doctors and superb team-mates in cricket. Now in business I have an accountant who is a genius, a brilliant legal expert and as before, superb team-mates. I guess the one advantage in business is that you can to a certain extent have control over who your team-mates are. You don't have to rely on the judgement of selectors.

My stories have taken me to many parts of Australia, and even overseas. They have given me the chance to stay in the best hotel rooms. I think it's a little bizarre that at top-level business conferences the two guys who get to stay in the classiest rooms are the head of the company and the guest speaker. I have had the chance to meet some of the business world's highest flyers. I just hope that I never forget that if I wasn't Mike Whitney, NSW and Australian cricketer, none of this would have happened. I owe the game of cricket a great deal.

One of the things I'm always asked when I agree to speak at a function is: 'What do you need?'

And I say: 'A stand-up mike.'

I always rely on my stories to get me through. When I'm

speaking, I like to take audiences right up, get them laughing and cheering . . . and then bring them back down with something a little bit heavy. That's what I've tried to do here in *Whiticisms* as well. I hope you get a good laugh with most of what's here, but I hope too that a few of the stories will make you think a bit about the game of cricket and maybe even a little bit about the game of life as well.

All of the stories that follow are fair dinkum, just like the stories I tell on stage. Perhaps I colour them up just a *fraction* occasionally, but basically this is how they happened. However I must confess there is one anecdote I sometimes relate at sports functions which is not exactly true. Well, I shouldn't say it's not true because no-one's ever told me it's false. However, the authenticity is questionable, so I won't put it among the chapters that follow. I'll put it right here instead. And I'd better leave the names out. For the sake of the story, we'll call our main character, an Englishman, 'Herbert'.

One year, Herbert travelled to Australia to play a season of grade cricket with a Sydney club, and while he was there the club organised a coaching clinic for the promising young cricketers from the local area. Inevitably a host of teenagers turned up, as did Herbert, dressed impeccably in English county cap, blue cravat, designer sunglasses, white tennis shirt and white tennis shorts. Rumour had it he had just ducked up after a spot of singles at White City tennis courts earlier that morning.

The youngsters were gathered into a group, and Herbert was introduced to them. He began his coaching school with a few batting hints. First lesson was the cover drive: 'Ah lads, when battin' get elbow up 'ere and front foot 'ere, and 'it through covers along ground. 'Cause if it's not along ground, you get caught, and if you get caught you're off ground, into pavilion and have cup o' tea with lads while your other mates bat. Now that's crap.'

He went through all the shots. Then it was the bowlers' turn.

'I hate you people!' he said. 'But anyway, get arm up 'ere, and 'ittin' seam and aimin' for that corridor of uncertainty . . .'

With that out of the way, Herbert sent the boys off to the nets. As those in the first batting group were getting themselves ready, he stood back behind where the faster bowlers would begin their run-ups, and lit his pipe. Behind him stood a posse of parents and friends, all anxious to see how their little Johnny or their neighbour's little Billy would go in front of the great Englishman.

In the far net was one little bloke who was determined to do well. Despite his size he saw himself as a quick bowler, and was charging in off a Dennis Lillee-length run-up and letting the ball go as fast as he could. But he was spraying them all over the place, and when he did happen to pitch a ball near the batsman he was duly smashed back out of the net. And to make matters worse, every time he ran in, he was accompanied by a loud, irritating, flapping sound. Soon Herbert could stand it no longer.

'Ah lad!' he called out. 'Ah, tiny lad in far net. Come 'ere.'

The little fella raced over. 'You're bowlin' rubbish, lad,' Herbert told him. 'And what's that flappin' sound every time you bowl?'

'Oh, I'm very sorry, sir,' the kid replied. 'But it's my boots. You see, I've had them for three seasons now, and they're coming apart where the stitching's gone.'

And then he showed where the sole of his right boot was all but separated from the rest.

'Oh dear,' said Herbert. 'Well, go back to yo' mark and concentrate on line and length.'

Sadly the kid's bowling did not improve, but the flapping sound grew louder and louder. The little bloke was such a trier, and everyone in the crowd of parents and onlookers felt desperately sorry for him. Within 10 minutes, Herbert had called him over again. This time he pulled him right away from all the other cricketers, over to a spot just in front of the gallery.

'Ah, lad, that flappin' is drivin' me mad.' Herbert muttered.
'I'm very sorry, sir.'

Herbert then did something that stunned the parents and friends, who were aware he had a reputation for being *extremely* careful with his money. He pulled out from the pocket of his tennis shorts the biggest wad of $100 bills anyone had ever seen. Then he pulled off the rubber band that was holding the notes together. You could hear the whispers through the gathering. Herbert was about to hand over a $100 bill so this gutsy little kid could have what he clearly couldn't afford — a new pair of cricket boots.

But if Herbert could hear the whispers, they made no difference. He handed the kid the rubber band.

'Ah lad,' Herbert said, 'put that around th'boot. That'll stop flappin' sound.'

•CHAPTER 1•

Introducing . . . Viv Richards

Wherever I do any public speaking these days, inevitably I get a heap of requests for my Viv Richards impersonation. I used to love watching him on the cricket field — the dominating way he batted, the things that he did . . . the (justified) arrogance of the man. He's an amazing character. I've seen him standing at first slip, arms crossed, staring away towards third man, with the bowler well into his delivery stride, but then . . . the snick comes and he snares it, no problem at all.

Unfortunately, such impersonations are more difficult on the printed page, so I won't even try to re-create the postures, the grunts, the waving, or the deep Antiguan accent. But I will tell you about the time my 'Viv' received its greatest acclaim.

To do so, I must tell you about the Australian cricket team's fines committee. On every Australian cricket tour, one of the first things the team has to do is form this committee — a three-man jury who have the task of recording all misdemeanours performed on tour and to hand out the appropriate penalties.

In the West Indies in 1991, the fines committee consisted of Tom Moody, David Boon and Ian Healy, three of the fairest, most honest, decent, worthy people you could ever meet. Fines meetings were conducted every couple of weeks and were held in conjunction with team meetings. A mega-fine was 20 US dollars, a standard fine two dollars, and all penalties were tallied up over the three months of the tour so that when we arrived in Bermuda at tour's end there was quite a kitty to splurge on team entertainment. Steve Waugh might have owed 10 dollars, Billy McDermott 15 dollars, Mike Veletta eight dollars, Merv Hughes 500 dollars . . . that sort of thing.

People were charged for anything: Getting a duck, being late, not wearing team uniform correctly . . . I remember one of the guys not wearing any jocks to a function (he wore the rest of his uniform, but no jocks) and that cost him five bucks. Another was chatted up by a transvestite but I can't recall what that cost him.

At a fines meeting the committee would hand down their rulings, after which they invited further accusations from the floor. Put simply, this was the chance to dob your mates in. But there was a catch — if your charge was ruled to be frivolous then you copped a fine yourself. For example, if I stood up and said, 'Mark Waugh combed his hair this morning, I think he should be fined,' the fines committee might go into conference and then announce: 'Roy, you've wasted two minutes of our time, that's cost you five US dollars.'

Of course, it's all done in good fun.

People have been fined for anything, even for getting hundreds. And, inevitably, not everyone agrees with the committee's ruling every time. Dean Jones *never* agreed. 'No, that wasn't the way it happened,' he would always say. Such were his protests, colleagues were trying to get him nabbed all the time. He would always challenge the fine . . . and the committee would always double it. His reaction to that was to abuse the fines committee, so he would be fined again. You can't swear at the fines committee.

The Test series in the Caribbean in '91 was decided in Barbados, where the Windies won the fourth Test to go two up in the series with only the Test in Antigua to play. After that fourth Test, at the post-match press conference, Viv Richards launched into this extraordinary tirade against Bob Simpson. It lasted for minutes and basically revolved around the fact that Simmo was 'not Viv's cup of tea'.

'He (Simmo) talks about me,' Viv said in a very angry tone, 'chasing after the umpire, but I remember in '78, you know, when Simpson was here with his team, and he was up (umpire Ralph) Gorien's nose every time. Don't give me this shit about Viv chasing umpires around . . .'

And so it went on. It was crazy.

I wasn't in the room when Viv ripped in, but I can remember the look on Simmo's face when he walked back into the Australian dressing room. He was ashen faced, and soon word started to filter through about Viv's tirade. Later that evening

I managed to get hold of a tape of the press conference, an event that led to my first ever Viv Richards impersonation. I played that tape over and over until I had the Antiguan accent okay; in fact by the time I was finished, not only did I know Viv's voice pretty well, I also knew what he had said about Simmo just about to the final angry syllable.

As soon as we arrived in Antigua, from Barbados, Ian Healy called a fines meeting. I got together with Heals and Tom Moody and asked them whether it might be a good idea to invite Viv along to say a few words. Relations between the teams hadn't been too flash and this seemed a way to smooth the waters. Heals knew what I was up to, and said, okay, bring him along.

I had one last listen to the tape of the press conference, borrowed a black stocking from one of the players' wives, pulled it over my face, and waited behind a curtain for my call.

Not long into the meeting, chairman Heals announced, straight-faced: 'Well, gentlemen, we have a special guest tonight. I've invited Viv Richards along.'

A couple of the blokes suddenly sat bolt upright. Billy McDermott couldn't believe it — Richards had been sledging him all tour. Likewise, Allan Border was stunned. He had played against Viv since 1979; there was no way the Windies captain would ever come to a function like this.

Out I came from behind the curtain. 'Well, it's nice for you, Heals, to invite me here,' 'Viv' began. ' 'Cause there's been too much animosity between the two teams . . .'

And then 'Viv' was into it. Everything he had said in Barbados came out again, word for word, every line delivered in the best impersonation I could muster — gestures, scowls (if it's possible to scowl behind a black stocking), body language, snorts, grunts, the lot.

I pulled it off. Simmo laughed himself hoarse; he thought it was really funny. At the end I received a standing ovation, and the guys were still chuckling days later. When I returned to

Australia, I introduced 'Viv' at my first speaking engagement and the audience thought it was great.

He's been one of the cornerstones of my public speaking escapades ever since.

•CHAPTER 2•

Hey Merv, Back Up the Truck!

When you travel overseas or interstate with cricket teams you get to room with a wide variety of people. While they all might be cricketers, they are all individuals, with vastly different tastes, habits and characteristics.

Take a bloke like Peter Taylor, farmer, off-spinner, extremely sensible man. With 'Motor', who I roomed with in Barbados on the 1991 West Indies tour, everything is always nice and neat. He runs his mornings like clockwork: up at 6.30, pre-breakfast cup of tea, down for the fair dinkum breakfast an hour later. You could set your watch by that first tinkle of teaspoon on the cuppa.

Rooming with Motor was a real buzz. As far as looking after the other guy, Motor was one of the greatest roomies of all time. He insisted the place was as tidy as his cricket bag, which was always immaculate. In Barbados, we stayed in these self-contained units that had their own kitchens, eating areas, and a separate room for one of us to sleep in (the other had to make do with the divan in the lounge room). Needless to say, Motor insisted I have the separate room. We had both been left out of the next Test and I suggested, to ease the pain of our non-selection, we have a couple of the team around for dinner.

'Splendid idea, Whits,' said Motor.

So off we went to the local supermarket, where we found a shopping trolley and headed for the aisles. This was an experience in itself. It was a bit like a mother and her son doing the grocery shopping. In my role as the son, I would be off ahead up the aisle grabbing everything off the shelves and tossing them in the trolley. Motor, as the mother, would then take out what I selected and place it back where it had come from.

'Whits, we don't need that, we only need this,' he'd scold.

We invited Mark Taylor and Mark Waugh around for dinner and, while Motor slaved over the roast chicken, I entertained the guests. It was a great night.

Motor and I had vastly different approaches to the morning. Now, I don't cope too well with them. However, on my first morning in Barbados, at some ungodly hour, I was woken by

a gentle tapping on my bedroom door and heard a voice, almost a whisper, from just outside my room: 'Roy . . . Roy . . .' was all it said.

'Whhaaattt!! Whhatttd'yaaawanttt??'

'Cup of tea and toast?'

Motor's a mate of mine, so I didn't say the first thing that came into my head. Instead I just rolled over. But 20 minutes later, there was that bloody tapping on the door again.

'Roy . . .'

'Oh, piss off Motor, will ya!'

And then I heard the door open and opened one eye just enough to see a ghostly figure with a cup of tea in one hand and a plate of toast in the other walk up to my bedside table. He placed them gently down, and then gave me a friendly pat on the shoulder.

'You'll be right, Whits,' I heard him say. 'Just have your cup of tea.'

And then he was gone.

Another thing I will never forget is ringing my mother from that unit in Barbados, and having a nice long chat with her. Afterwards Motor said to me: 'Were you yelling out to your mother in Australia then, or were you just talking on the phone?'

I don't know why it is, but whenever I make a long-distance phone call, I feel obliged to push the decibels up a few notches when I'm speaking, as if to compensate for the many kilometres between myself and the person I'm talking to. Am I the only person that does that?

Another amusing phone conversation I once had occurred a lot closer to home, in Adelaide. I was rooming with Mark Waugh, and one day, when I answered the phone, a young girl's voice was on the other end.

'Oh, hello,' said the young lady, 'can I please speak to Mark Waugh?'

'Who's speaking, please?' I'd ask.

'Oh . . . oh, you don't know me,' she said.

And I replied: 'Well, this is Mark speaking.'

'Ahh, well, you don't know me. My name's Melissa . . .'

At about this point I interrupted: 'Oh, excuse me, I've got to be honest. My name's Mike Whitney. I'm the Australian fast bowler.'

'Oh,' said Melissa.

That was all she said. And then after a brief pause . . .

'Goodbye.'

Junior was a very easy-going roomie, which suited me fine. Of course, not everyone's like that. I can remember sharing with Geoff Lawson in about 1981 or 1982, and being told by my more senior fast bowling partner that he liked to sleep with the blinds open . . . and the radio on. After one night of this I'd had enough. I said: 'Listen, "Henry", you're going to have to make a choice. Either you can have the blinds open, OR the radio on. I don't care which, but not both.'

He really got shitty. I think the radio won out in the end. I thought at this point that he might be the roomie from Hell, but he turned out to be outstanding. I roomed with Henry for a long time and we became great mates.

One time when Henry and I had a bit of a 'blue' occurred not long after he was appointed captain of NSW. It was Wayne 'Cracker' Holdsworth's debut match, in 1988–89, and Cracker started with a bang. He grabbed two wickets in his first over in first-class cricket, and 6–50 for the innings. I remember looking over at him in the dressing room and saying: 'I've played first-class cricket for seven or eight years and my best bowling figures are 6–64. You've been playing five minutes and you've beaten me.'

We took Cracker out that night . . . and made a mess of him. I felt six wickets in your debut innings was more than sufficient cause for a big celebration. Because Cracker was the new boy in the team he was rooming with the captain, which created something of a problem at 5.30 the next morning when it was time to bring him home. I'd had a couple, but . . . you know, the old bull and the young bull . . . I was okay. Cracker was a soft banana. I knocked on our leader's door and announced: 'He's home, Henry!' Then I left Cracker leaning up against the door.

The next day, I copped a blast from Henry in front of the whole team. But afterwards he pulled me aside. All he said was: 'You know, Roy, I had to do that.'

One of the best blokes I ever roomed with was Shane Warne. We shared a room in Sri Lanka in 1992, a time I'll never forget if only for one of the most bizarre things that I ever saw while touring.

One morning, Shane woke and noticed a little accumulation of dust or dirt, right next to his pillow. He said, just a little nervously: 'Big Roy, take a look at that . . . there's a pile of dirt right in front of my nose.'

I got out of bed, but I couldn't work it out. It was like someone had ashed a cigar in that exact spot. 'I don't know, mate, maybe there's something in that mattress,' was the best I could do.

So Warney had the hotel staff change the mattress. But next morning, there it was again — this little pile of dirt about 10 centimetres from Shane's eyebrows, which had somehow got there while he slept. What could we do? Shane blew it away, but by the next morning, when it was there again, he was just about spooked. When he next went to bed on that mattress he was not sleeping too close to that spot. He was jammed against the wall, hoping that whatever was leaving that dirt near his nose would at least leave him alone.

When the dirt was back the next morning, Warney rang the lobby to abuse the staff for replacing the mattress with the same mattress. Which they denied. So we stayed and watched them replace the mattress with a third one. But it didn't do any good. When Warney woke the following morning, there it was again!

I'd wake up in the morning and watch Shane. He'd open just one eye, and look for the little circle of dirt.

'Shit, it's there again!'

Finally we turned our attention to the roof. It had never occurred to us, but up there was a little patch, in just the right spot, that wasn't a hole but had worn thinner than the rest of the ceiling. We called in the hotel staff again, and organised for a bloke to come in and patch up the spot. Which he did.

Even that didn't work. Next day . . . there it was again. We never did find out what caused it. It probably would have made a fairly decent practical joke, but if one of the team was putting the dirt there they never owned up to it. Our guess was it was an animal of some description scuffing away on the roof every night. But we never heard it, and I can tell you, we listened.

I enjoyed rooming with Warney. He is a bloke with a lot of energy, and that tour of Sri Lanka was a very interesting time in his career. He began that tour with hardly a Test wicket to his name, but it was in the first Test that he had his first international success. From that point, he progressively developed into a superstar.

Shane is now well versed in some of the procedures that recur on tours — things such as the room allocations, at which you find out who your next roomie will be. I can remember how things were in my days in the Test squad. The entire team would stand around in a nervous group, waiting to see who they would be sharing the next few days with. Then the manager steps forward with the announcements.

'Shane Warne and Steve Waugh, room 214 . . .'

'Mark Taylor and Ian Healy . . . room 226 . . .'

'Allan Border . . . 240 . . .'

'Merv Hughes . . .'

Everyone cringes . . .

'. . . and Mike Whitney . . .'

The room number is lost in a wild celebration as the remaining guys cheer and punch the air. Meanwhile, my whole world has collapsed around me and then suddenly, I am grabbed in a massive headlock.

'MATEY!!!'

It's my new roomie.

Not long after my team-mates finished wishing me the best of luck, we'd head up to our room. Inevitably there would be one double and one single bed. Now whereas Peter Taylor would unselfishly offer you the double, Merv's bags were on there in a flash.

'And where are you gonna sleep, Big Roy?' I can still hear Merv saying.

That room draw is not the only ballot Australian cricketers of the late '80s and early '90s came to dread. The worse seat in the plane was always the one directly in front of Merv. If you were in seat 19A and Merv drew 20A you knew it was going to be a long flight. Within seconds of takeoff, maybe even before takeoff, a long hairy arm would reach over from behind you and grab your hair, which in my case, of course, was a curly mop. It attracted him like a magnet.

'MATEY!!!' he'd bellow. 'ARE WE GOING TO HAVE A GOOD TIME!!!'

That was a statement, not a question. Then he'd stick a finger in my ear . . .

'HEY, WHAT'S HAPPENING, WHITS!!!'

Or he'd lick my ear, or give me a big, sloppy kiss on the cheek. Those kisses! I remember one season, Allan Border had to miss a couple of one-day internationals because he was suffering from swimmer's ear. All caused because Merv had kissed him too much. Poor AB had to run away in the end, or stay in the huddle and give a quick pep-talk with his hands over his ears.

After a long flight during a tour, the first thing I'd usually do was head for the shower. Not Merv, he'd head for the phone and call room service. I've seen Merv walk into a hotel room and immediately set about memorising the room service menu, so he wouldn't have to worry about looking at it again.

While I'm in the shower I'd hear Merv yell out: 'Hey, Big Roy, do you want anything from room service?'

'No,' I'd reply, 'we're having dinner in an hour.'

'But you've gotta have something.'

'No thanks, mate.'

'Big Roy!!'

It was as if he needed an excuse to make the call. More as a way of shutting him up, I'd concede: 'Okay, get me a milk-shake and a toasted sandwich.'

And then he'd be on the phone. When I stepped out of the shower, Merv was ready to hop in, so it was my job to greet the guy who delivered the order. Which was enormous. It was never a couple of sangers and a couple of milkshakes. It was a couple of trolleys. Merv would take it upon himself to sample the entire menu, plus every flavour of milkshake . . . with and without malt. And then he'd be out of the shower, wrapped only in one of those tiny hotel towels, to make sure nothing had been forgotten.

He is the unchallenged king of eating. The first time I ever saw him in action was in Darwin, where he ruined a guy who ran a smorgasbord in one of the local hotels. I'll never forget the excited look on his face the morning after he first went there. 'Big Roy,' he said, 'you've gotta come to this place. It's 20 bucks and BACK UP THE TRUCK!'

All the buffets we ever ventured to were known as 'Back up the trucks'. He'd say that every time. 'What's on tonight?' he might ask on tour, and someone would reply: 'Oh, we're going to a smorgasbord . . .'

'You beauty,' Merv would roar. 'BACK UP THE TRUCK!'

We were in Darwin to assist with a coaching clinic, and the first thing I saw Merv do was walk up to one of the students in a net, carrying a broom in his right hand. Why, I asked, did he have a broom with him?

'I'm gonna show the kid how to play the sweep shot,' he explained.

He was actually going in to get some grass off the artificial wicket, but I liked his explanation better. That was typical Merv humour . . . off the cuff, always said with a cheeky grin, always funny.

I love the guy.

• CHAPTER 3 •

How Steve Waugh Caned the Toads

One of the most important characteristics of every cricketer who played in the NSW Shield teams of my era was the fierce pride they had in their origins. We were all extremely proud New South Welshmen and cherished our baggy blue caps.

No-one exudes that pride more than Stephen Waugh. He loves the fact he's from NSW, and doesn't mind letting people know, especially when the Blues are going well on the paddock. In the Australian dressing room, Steve's forever geeing up his good friend Ian Healy about the fact that while NSW has won 41 Sheffield Shields, Queensland haven't been *quite* that successful, and between 1992 and 1994 he was pretty keen to remind Heals that Queensland (the 'Cane Toads') lost three straight State of Origin rugby league series to NSW (the 'Cockroaches'). Heals loves the league and is a very committed Brisbane Broncos fan, and he didn't need anyone, especially Steve Waugh, reminding him that until their win in 1995, Queensland hadn't won an Origin series since 1991, the year the great Queensland five-eighth 'King' Wally Lewis retired from representative football.

Stephen is such a gifted sportsman, I reckon he could have been a success at just about any ball sport he had chosen. I love him, and rate him as just about my favourite all-time cricketer. There might have been classier batsmen, but Stephen's my fave.

I'll tell you two truly amazing stories Stephen's wife, Lynette, related one day over dinner, both of which have a very special significance for me following the birth of our triplets. You hear tales of twins possessing a kind of telepathy, whereby they know what's happening to their sibling even though they may be great distances apart. I'm intrigued as to whether my children are going to have that gift. So I asked — had the telepathy thing ever happened to Steve and Mark.

Lynette told me a story that when Mark was going through a horror stretch in Sri Lanka in 1992, she and Steve were holidaying in America. For some reason, the selectors had left Stephen out of the Australian touring team. One day, in a hotel room in the States, Steve jumped out of bed, turned to Lynette and said: 'Mark got a pair last night.'

Simple as that. And yep, you guessed it, it was true.

Lynette also recalled another occasion when Steve calmly announced that Mark had just made a big score. Junior was playing county cricket with Essex at the time, and had, in fact, belted a double century.

I can remember a game where Mark got out hooking at a time when NSW were in a fair bit of trouble. That was the third or fourth wicket to fall before lunch on the opening day; it was a disastrous dismissal for us and looked a dumb way to get out. In the dressing room, as the shot was played, I spat out: 'You're kidding, Junior! What a bloody stupid way to go.'

Right next to me was brother Stephen, and he was into me: 'Hey, don't you bag him,' he roared. 'You never complain when he plays those shots and they go for four. You're the first one clapping, aren't you.'

An outburst like that is not usually Stephen's go. 'Mate,' I said, 'look at the situation of the . . .'

'When he gets a 50 or a 100,' Steve continued, still in a very angry tone, 'you're up there punching the air.'

And then he just walked away and left me there.

After lunch, Steve grabbed a bag of balls, gave me a nudge, and asked if I wanted to go out to the nets for a bowl. Which I did. Once there, he apologised for 'flying off the handle'. It was cool, I told him, and anyway, he was right. I had no right to shoot off at Mark like that.

'You've got to understand.' Steve Waugh said to me: 'We're very close.'

More often the impression they leave is of two vastly differ-ent characters, with little in common. They don't even look alike. Mark's taller, thicker in the hips with that big arse of his, while Stephen's is more the slim body of a natural athlete.

Watch them when they bat together — they very rarely have mid-wicket conferences. Many times during my career, when the twins were batting, I would sit in the dressing room and speculate on when they'd next get together for a chat between overs. An over would end, and both would walk towards the middle of the pitch. But neither Waugh would be looking at the other. Occasionally one might stop to pat down the wicket; the other might take a quick peek at the scoreboard. Still, they'd get closer, until they were almost together in mid-pitch. The wicket would receive one more encouraging tap . . . and then they'd turn back towards their respective ends. Not a word, not even a glance, had been exchanged.

I asked Steve one day whether the telepathy that exists between them means that they don't need to talk out there in the centre; that they know how the other is thinking so there is no need for a conference.

'Oh yeah, a lot of times we don't even call,' Steve replied.

'Which probably explains,' I commented, 'why you get run out all the time!'

Steve let that one go through to the keeper.

While they're certainly good mates off the field, you would

never call them inseparable. One day, after Steve had headed off in one direction and Mark was about to go in another, I said to Mark: 'How come you and Stephen don't hang out together?'

He turned to me and said: 'I lived with him in the same room for 20 years, Big Roy. Why do I want to hang around with him now?'

Stephen doesn't mind the physical sports, which is a bit different to Mark. When we used to play touch footy, I'd give Mark one in the ribs, and it'd be: 'Eh, careful! We're only playing touch. We're not playing tackle.' But Stephen, you give him a little tickle and he'll just look at you. You know he'd be lining you up. And he'd get you back, no problem.

Steve's a great inventor of games. During a rained-out match, he would suddenly emerge with a putter and two golf balls.

MARK & STEVE WAUGH.

Who knows where he found them. Within minutes the SCG dressing room had been converted into a makeshift nine-hole putt-putt course. All the kits were organised. You have to get the ball between Mo Matthews' boots over there — that's hole one. Then down the stairs that lead out onto the playing area and, if the rain's eased off, out onto the field, back through the gate. If there was no-one around we might have ventured into the Members' bar. And finally back to where we started. The ninth green is always near the first tee on a fair dinkum golf course. So it is at the SCG.

The best performance as a double act I've ever seen from the pair came in Perth, in a Sheffield Shield match in 1990–91. The WA attack we faced that day was a bloody good one — Terry Alderman, Bruce Reid, Chris Matthews, Ken Macleay, Tom Moody — and the pitch had something in it. Geoff Marsh, the opposing skipper, sent us in, and soon after lunch we were a little shaky, at 4–137.

Thirteen minutes less than seven hours batting time later, Geoff Lawson declared at 4–601. Mark was 229 not out, Steve 216 not out. Neither had offered a chance! The first-class cricket records broken were amazing — a world partnership record for the fifth wicket, a Sheffield Shield partnership record for any wicket, the highest partnership for any wicket by two Australians, the highest ever by two brothers (let alone twins!), the first time two brothers had scored double centuries in the same innings, the first stand over 400 by two NSW batsmen. And on and on and on . . .

It was one of the great privileges of my career to be able to see that partnership. It was just awesome.

Henry waited until Steve and Mark had passed the Shield partnership record (which had been held by David Hookes and Wayne Phillips) before closing the innings. They were on fire at the time, so delaying a little wasn't going to cost us much time. As it was the declaration came about 45 minutes before tea.

The contrast in the thinking of the two of them when they

came back to the dressing room said a lot about their different characters. Mark walked in and accepted the cheers, the applause and the pats on the back with his usual nonchalance. He went over to his kit, sat down, put his helmet down beside him and quietly took off his gloves and placed them back in their rightful spot in his kit. Then he stood up, walked over to a mirror and gave his haircut a long look. There might have been one or two locks out of place, so he gave them a flick back to where they belonged, and then ran his fingers through the mane to recreate that casual, elegant look. Satisfied, he strolled back over to his spot on the bench. Things were cool.

'Gee, you're looking all right today,' someone commented.

'Oh yeah,' he grinned back. 'Not bad.'

Stephen was a little different. His kit was parked next to mine in the dressing room. You knew it was his because it was in its usual state of disarray, gear spraying out in all directions. I was sitting there lacing up my boots in preparation for my first shot at the Sandgropers when he stormed into the room . . . and threw his bat down in the direction of his bag.

'I can't believe we've declared!' he complained loud enough for everyone to hear. Our captain, Geoff Lawson, didn't say anything, but I couldn't let it go. 'What's wrong with you?' I asked. 'You probably wanted to declare as well,' he muttered, 'so you can have a bloody bowl.'

I said, as calmly as I could: 'That's a pretty selfish attitude, isn't it? You've just put on a world record partnership. My hands are sore from clapping and you're whingeing about Henry declaring!'

He looked up at me, without a hint of a smile, and said: 'But we could have put on 600.'

I wasn't really sure what to say after that. 'You selfish bastard,' I sneered at him, 'I can't believe you said that.'

'What's your problem?' he said.

'Well,' I said, 'You and your bloody brother have just gone out and scored 464 in less than seven hours, and you're not bloody satisfied. All you can do is complain. I haven't scored 464 in my whole career!'

Yet you know, despite what I said, in many ways I loved the way he had reacted. To me, it summed up the Steve Waugh approach to the game. He's never satisfied, always wants more.

A not-so-well-known fact is Stephen's role in my most important performance in Test cricket, the 7–89 against the West Indies in Adelaide in 1989. During that match, I grew inwardly as a person nine times. It was just such a big turning point in my career, and my life.

In the nets the day before the game, I was bowling with an old ball, and getting the thing to move away in the air just a bit from the right-handers, with what we call 'Irish' or reverse swing. Steve said to me: 'If you bowl that stuff in the game, that line and that length, you'll get wickets.'

'You reckon?' I said.

'Mate, don't worry about this swinging-it-in crap they keep talking about,' he said. 'If you keep angling it across, and getting a bit of movement, they won't be able to help themselves.'

At the time a few people had been bagging my selection, basing much of that criticism on my alleged lack of an inswinger. I must admit the knockers had got at me a little, and even though I knew I had the inswinger in my armoury if I needed it, my confidence had been dented.

But Stephen set me straight, and I went into the match with a very positive attitude. The result was a seven-for and a two-for for M. Whitney, and all from going across them and swinging it away. Every time I took a wicket, Stephen was there, patting me on the back, telling me he knew I could do it.

In St Kitts on the 1991 Aussie tour of the West Indies, Stephen and I had a night out on which we visited a local resort for a few drinks and a meal. We didn't head there until after the sun had set, which created some problems, because the island was absolutely littered with cane toads. You'd have sworn it was a part of Queensland. St Kitts depends on sugar cane for much of its export income and consequently the place is loaded with these toads, which can grow up to be pretty big boys. They love to come out at night, and created an extraordinary sight on the nine-hole golf course which was located just across from where we were staying. Once dusk arrived the course would be covered, wall to wall, by a carpet of toads. You couldn't have dragged a buggy up the fairway.

Both on the way to the resort, and then again on our way home we were continually sidestepping the toads that crowded the footpaths.

It was on our return trip that a huge, gigantic, *enormous* cane toad suddenly jumped out into our path. Now, you have to understand that before my arrival in St Kitts, I'd never even seen a cane toad, let alone come face to face with the mother of them all. With their big guts, multiple chins and bulging eyes, they are just about the ugliest creatures God ever created, and when they're as big as this monster they can slow you down just a fraction. When this bastard jumped in front of us, I retreated back a pace or three, to let the thing go about its business.

Not Stephen. As soon as he saw it, he reacted like the soccer centre forward he could well have been. He launched into this huge kick that sent the big toad spinning though the moonlight into a hedge on the other side of the road. It was an absolute classic. One second, I'm jumping out of the way fearing for my life, the next the cause of my concern is flying through the air looking about as dangerous as a tadpole in a shark tank.

As the cane toad sailed off into the distance, Steve followed its path with a satisfied grin. And when it crashed into the hedge he couldn't help himself. If only Ian Healy had been there, to see Steve shout out to the helpless toad: 'Get that up ya, King Wally!'

•CHAPTER 4•

Dressing Up For the Australian Cricketers

It was in St Kitts and then again in Jamaica that we experienced for the first time the unusual but highly effective technique of petrol being used as a means of drying the wicket. Every day of the three-day game in St Kitts a huge black cloud would form in the distance, and at around 2pm it would come over and dump a tropical storm's worth of water all over the ground.

On one of the three days, the groundsman didn't get the covers out in time and the square was saturated. His solution? As soon as the storm cleared, he strolled out to the middle with a big metal tin and a tea cup, and started pouring the contents of the tin over the pitch, using the cup to make sure the liquid was evenly spread. We didn't know what was going on. Then he lit the pitch. Whooosh! Within seconds, this huge black cloud of smoke was billowing up off the centre of the ground.

It didn't take long for the fire to burn itself out. Then the groundsman brought his broom and roller out. The sweeping and rolling took about 10 minutes, after which the pitch was rock, rock hard. Play was under way within 20 minutes of the first raindrop hitting the square.

By Jamaica, we were used to this sort of thing. What I'll always remember about the pitch at Sabina Park in Kingston was its appearance the day before the Test began. It was grassless and rock hard. At practice, we noticed the groundsman was giving the wicket a nice long drink. I thought this was a good idea but our batsmen were horrified. Then the curator grabbed a bucket of hay and, as he strode down the side of the pitch, tossed the contents of the bucket high in the air and watched it settle on the wicket. Ten minutes later, he grabbed the roller and rolled the hay into the pitch.

By the time we'd completed our session, the wicket was rock solid again with the rolled-in hay giving it a much whiter look than it had had before the groundsman's efforts. The following day, it played okay, perhaps a little low if anything.

In St Kitts, the ground we played on backed onto the local prison. So, who better to give the groundsman a hand with the less exciting jobs than the local prisoners? When we first arrived to have a net at the ground, I was taken by the sight of about 20 of the groundstaff, who I didn't realise then were doing time, rolling the wicket (the roller had no motor, you had to push it) while others trimmed the outfield with tiny pairs of scissors.

The guys operating the roller and cutting the outfield all wore the same gear — overalls that were dark bluish with, can you believe it, light blue arrows on them! The gear looked like something out of one of those old Bugs Bunny cartoons. I noticed that some of the guys were working a lot harder than others. Some of the blokes rolling the pitch were putting in the hard yards, but others were lifting no more than a finger. I assumed they were the foremen.

There was one guy standing on his own wearing what appeared to be a guard's outfit. He sported a badge on his uniform, and had a machine gun at the ready. I went over for a chat.

Before I relate my conversation with this gentleman, I must explain that there are two types of people in the Caribbean. Firstly, there are the one-word West Indians, such as Curtly Ambrose . . .

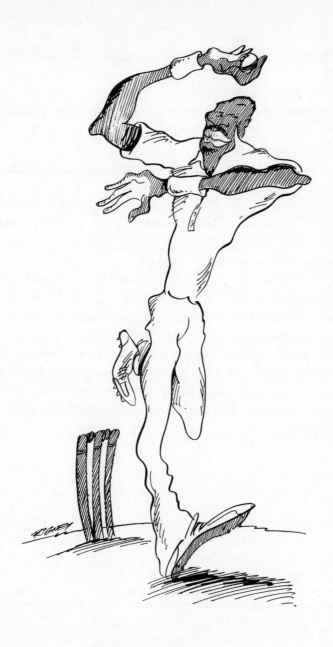

CURTLY AMBROSE

I'll say g'day to Curtly: 'How you goin', Curtly?'
'Cool.'
Nothing more. Just 'cool'.
And then there are the West Indians who take a little *more* than one word. Such as Brian Lara.
'How you goin', Brian?'
'Oh, I'm cool, Whitty, what's happenin' man? Isn't life beautiful. How you goin' . . .'
And on he goes. Well, this prison guard turned out to be a one-word West Indian. There he stood, uniform, badge, machine gun.
'Hey, are you a warden?' I asked.
He turned around to me and replied: 'You stupid?'
That stopped me for a second. Then I asked: 'What about these guys cutting the outfield with the little scissors?'
'Oh, they in big trouble. They in for life.'
It was then I realised they were inmates from the local prison. 'Well, what about the overalls they're wearing,' I continued. 'You know, I've never seen anything like them before.'
'Oh, they special. Today they get dressed up for the Australian cricketers.'

•CHAPTER 5•

Over and Out!

I was in the Sabina Park dressing room in Kingston, Jamaica, getting ready for my first innings in a Test match for more than two years. This was the first Test of the Australia–West Indies series of 1991, a contest recognised by everyone as the cricket championship of the world. I wasn't nervous . . . yet. After all, Australia had just gone seven wickets down and M. Whitney was going in at number 11, so there was no point getting too worried about things just at that moment. Billy McDermott had gone out to the middle to join David Boon, who was playing another superb and courageous dig. And Merv Hughes was still to bat before I would get my turn.

As I prepared to strap my pads on, I looked down at my collection of protective equipment. I had the full complement — more than I'd ever had before: Pads, gloves, helmet, thigh guard, inside-leg thigh guard, arm-guard, chest guard, protector, two pairs of football socks to stuff in my protector. You needed all this gear and more. I remembered facing Patrick Patterson in a game at St Kitts and being hit on the pad by a couple of lightning quick deliveries. Days later I still had the bruises.

Every so often (more accurately about every 60 seconds) the quiet of the dressing room was interrupted by the frenzied roar of the crowd. This might have meant a wicket had fallen, or it might have meant another bouncer had been bowled. The Caribbean crowd was like that, they'd yell for just about anything. I slowly reached for my front pad, to strap onto my leg, when I heard the sound of footsteps running down into the dressing room. It was our 12th man, Stephen Waugh.

'You'd better hurry up, Whit,' he said, 'Merv's out.'

Merv's *out*? I didn't even realise he was in!

I know it's etiquette to pass the incoming batsman at the gate, but this time there was a good 90-seconds gap between Merv leaving the field and Michael Whitney appearing. The delay had only helped to set the scene, like a 15-minute break before a football grand final, and my arrival was greeted in a way the crowds must have greeted the Christians as they were led into the Colosseum.

'Whooaaa!!' roared the locals. 'Kill 'im as well!!'

I gazed up on the scoreboard and the first thing I saw was 'D Boon . . . 106'. I thought: 'Thank God he's got his hundred.' If he was on 99 his chances of getting three figures wouldn't have been too good. I was, after all, going to be on strike . . . facing Patrick Patterson.

When I reached the middle and before I asked for guard, I looked at Boonie. But he wasn't looking at me, he was looking at the groundstaff out on the edge of the boundary. Here they were, waiting to come out and work on the wicket. One of the crew was already trying to kick start the motor on the roller. The chief groundsman was standing there with his paintbrush dripping with fresh white paint, all ready to re-mark the popping creases! This was not a confidence booster.

The West Indies had just taken the new ball. Why is it that teams, especially West Indian Test teams with big nasty fast bowlers like Patrick Patterson, always take the second new ball when numbers nine, 10 and 11 are due at the wicket? And especially when M. Whitney is playing against them? Fair dinkum, I reckon I've faced more new balls than some opening batsmen I've played with.

Boonie walked up and said: 'Just concentrate on the ball, that's the most important thing. Patrick's only bowling seamers.'

'Seamers!!' I replied calmly.

'Oh well . . . *fast* seamers.'

Then my little Tasmanian mate repeated: 'Just concentrate on the ball, and you'll be okay . . .'

Followed by: 'Otherwise you're gonna get hurt.'

I've never forgotten that.

I took centre and then took a quick stroll to pat the pitch down a bit. From first slip came this from Viv: 'We're not making no Tooheys ad today, Whitty.' And they're all laughing.

Then the crowd started chanting: 'Pat-TRICK! . . . Pat-TRICK! . . . Pat-TRICK! . . .'

After a little bit of this (about 30 seconds) I realised it wasn't 'Pat-TRICK' they were chanting. It was 'Hat-TRICK'!

'Hat-TRICK! . . . Hat-TRICK! . . . Hat-TRICK! . . .'

'Hey Babs,' I whispered as loudly as I could, 'is Patterson on a bloody hat-trick?'

Boonie just smiled. I didn't know until this moment that Billy and Merv had been dismissed by successive deliveries. I began thinking along the lines of: 'I don't want to be remembered as the third leg of Patrick Patterson's Test hat-trick. You can take seven or eight wickets in a Test innings but that'll be forgotten if you're the third leg of Patrick Patterson's Test hat-trick. I don't want that.'

By this point Patterson was just about to start his long run and as he set off the crescendo began to build up . . . and build up. Soon he was steaming in, and I'm thinking: 'Concentrate . . . concentrate . . . concentrate . . . CONCENTRATE.' But that was the one thing I was definitely not doing. About halfway in, I said to myself: 'You're in trouble, mate, you're not concentrating.'

So, two steps from the delivery stride, I bailed out. I put my left hand up like a traffic cop and walked away towards the square-leg umpire. The crowd went mad. Patterson didn't let go of the ball, but he still followed through and ended up about two or three metres from where I was standing. He was spewing, but he didn't say anything to me. He did, however, say plenty to his captain. From what I could gather from the commotion behind the wicket, Viv wasn't too happy either.

The booing and hissing went on for a little while, and then the entire process that had led up to Patterson's aborted first delivery was repeated. I walked down the wicket and gave the pitch a nudge. The crowd resumed its 'HAT-trick!' chant. Boonie gave me a grin. Viv said something about the bloody Tooheys ad. The eight fieldsmen behind the wicket all laughed again.

Patterson finally returned to his bowling mark and charged in again. When he bowled, I was as ready as I could be . . . and leaned back to avoid the inevitable bouncer. I think I ducked as well. But Patrick hadn't read the script. He bowled a bloody yorker, which made a complete fool out of me, but missed the off stump by a coat of varnish.

I saw the video of that delivery later and Greg Chappell was commentating for Channel Nine. 'I'm not quite sure what Mike Whitney was doing there ducking a yorker,' said Greg.

Viv was really pissed off. He knew that if that ball had been on the stumps, the innings was over. He decided to change his field. Gus Logie was moved a little closer at short leg. Richie Richardson was brought up into a very short cover position. Dessie Haynes joined Logie in close on the leg side.

I didn't have to be Einstein to figure out where the next was going. Up my hooter, that's where. There were no two ways about that. With all these guys surrounding me, I knew their job was to catch either the ball that rebounded off the helmet or the one that hit up near the splice of the bat.

Patterson roared in and fired the ball into the pitch. I was swaying back out of the way, but the ball followed me and all I could do was play this self-preservation type jab at the ball to prevent it catching me on the chin. Fortunately the ball hit the bat . . . and lobbed straight over Richardson and out to the conventional spot for the cover fieldsman. But, of course, there was no-one in the covers. There was no-one even close to the ball. Which meant a single, and the bowler's end. You bewdy!!

'YEESSSSSSSSSSS!!!'

No-one tried to prevent the single, but I still ran about 30 metres past the stumps at the bowler's end, just in case Boonie had any thoughts of two. At that point, even though I'd only been out there for five minutes, I felt like I was in the middle of the longest innings of my life. I'd thwarted the hat-trick ball, I'd even scored a run and I had sweat pouring off me. I grabbed at the strap of my helmet and took my lid off, not to acknowledge the crowd, just to cool off a bit, but then looked around me and saw that almost every West Indian was changing his

position in the field. After my initial surprise, I realised such a strategy made sense, as Boonie was past his century. I took my gloves off, and as I did so I heard this laughter coming from just behind me. I turned around, and the bloke chuckling was Steve Bucknor, the umpire.

'What are you laughing at?' I asked.

The ump suddenly turned serious. 'I've got some bad news for you, Mr Whitney,' Bucknor said. And then he started laughing again, his pearly white teeth glistening in the sun.

'That is over!!'

This was the low point of my career. The bowler at the other end was Courtney Walsh. I decided, bugger this, I'm going down swinging, so to his first delivery to me, I gave myself a bit of room, swung as hard as I could, and edged the ball down to fine leg. Another single! Who was laughing now? But, would you believe it, Boonie just blocked the remaining five balls of the over. At the end of it, I marched up the pitch to find out what was going on and Boonie just grinned again and said: 'Oh, mate, I just wanted to watch you facing Patterson again.'

About two balls into the over, Patterson knocked my middle peg cartwheeling out of the ground. 'Thank God for that!' I thought. Tub Taylor was waiting for me at the gate applauding: 'Gutsy effort, Roy,' he said. 'You've done us proud.'

I said to him: 'Gee, Tubs, I don't know how that one got through.'

He suggested I look at the replay. They had this old black-and-white TV set in the away dressing room, and through the mist on the screen I noticed that, as the ball arrived, you could have driven a car through the gap between my bat and pad. I'd retreated to the leg-side and then pushed out my bat without ever even thinking of moving my pads anywhere near the line of the ball.

Funny . . . it didn't seem like that when I was out there in the middle.

• CHAPTER 6 •

A Caribbean Picnic

I don't know whether cricket fans in Australia appreciate just what our batsmen go through on a tour of the West Indies. I know it was tough in 1991, and from watching the 1995 series on television, it seemed that nothing had changed. The painful reality of the batsmen's task was brought home to me in no uncertain terms when I batted on the second day of the Guyana Test of the 1991 tour.

I was facing Malcolm Marshall, one of the game's all-time great fast bowlers, who was perhaps a little below his absolute best on that tour, but was still an excellent, very rapid and very dangerous bowler. His first ball to me was pitched up and it hit me smack on the shin, fairly adjacent to the stumps. My first reaction was 'that's out', and I soon realised Marshall felt exactly the same way.

He didn't so much appeal as head towards the dressing sheds. But I looked up and the ump had given me not out. 'Oh, no,' I thought. 'Here we go.'

Marshall couldn't believe it and neither could his team-mates. One of them asked me why I wasn't walking, which would have set a lovely precedent — walking on a lbw. Mind you, after looking at the expression on Marshall's face and having given due consideration to my health, strolling off in a gesture of sportsmanship might not have been a bad idea.

The next one was going to be a shortie for sure. I was ducking not long after he started his run, but it didn't get up like I needed it to, and instead of sailing over my head and through to Jeffrey Dujon behind the stumps it struck me a glancing blow on the ribcage and flew down to fine leg for a leg bye. Or so I thought. The umpire, who only a minute earlier had condemned me to Malcolm Marshall at his angriest, now ruled this was a dead ball, not a leg bye, and I had to stay at the batsman's end. How he ruled that way I will never, ever know. The rule book says that if a batsman is struck while trying to avoid a delivery then any resultant leg byes are valid. Did the ump really believe I wasn't going to try and dodge a Malcolm Marshall fast one aimed right at my body?

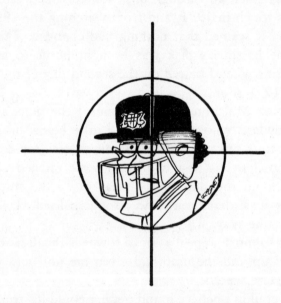

WEST INDIES FAST BOWLER'S
VIEW OF AN AUSSIE TAILENDER

Soon afterwards the innings ended, and we had to bowl for the rest of the day, during which time Richie Richardson and Dessie Haynes gave us a fair bit of stick. I didn't think anything of that non-leg-bye until I showered after stumps. Where Marshall had nicked me, I had developed a big, nasty bruise. I hadn't even felt it when it struck. I had seen the battle scars worn by our batsmen during the series; now I had one of my own.

Our specialist batsmen were battered and bruised by the end of that tour. In fact, I'm probably right in saying that when we arrived in Bermuda after the serious side of the tour had ended there wasn't one guy in the squad who didn't have a problem with his fingers or hands: busted fingers, swollen joints — from getting struck on the gloves, time and time again. They were on the back foot, bumper after bumper, ball after ball.

Every team in the West Indies has a collection of fast bowlers. They vary in quality, but they all have them. A heap of them can bowl quick, but not all of them can bowl straight and not all of them can bowl smart. Jamaica had a big left-arm fellow who took a few wickets — I remember he knocked AB over and ran four laps of the ground — but he was all over the place, while at the other end was Courtney Walsh, just as quick and always on the spot.

There was a bloke called Tony Gray, about 200cm tall, who took six wickets in one of the limited-overs internationals but who on the whole wasn't very impressive. He could bowl a majestic spell but the next day get carted all over the ground. At one point, after Gray had said something out on the paddock, AB called him a 'reject county bowler', which was a real good sledge.

I can recall the Australian team playing a game against a West Indies under-23s side in St Vincent, and Mark Taylor saying to everyone before he went out to bat: 'I'm really looking forward to this, a chance to open up against something other than sheer bloody pace. This should be a real chance to get a nice long hit.'

The Windies under-23s were led by Brian Lara, but we didn't know any of their bowlers so it was little wonder Tubs assumed he'd be in for an easier time. At lunch Mark was no more than 30 not out, and was battered and bruised after facing a barrage from three young punks I know he'll never forget. They were like lightning! I should add that Tubs went on to get 122, but the thing I'll always remember is his comment when he came in for lunch.

'Bloody hell,' he said through gritted teeth, 'some picnic that was!'

Mind you, it wasn't just on the field that we had our problems in the Caribbean. Even the simplest things sometimes caused moments of stress. I remember a cab trip in Kingston, Jamaica, that cost me 100 Jamaican dollars when it should have cost me 20. I'd completed the journey the day before and it had cost me 20 bucks, but when I did the trip the second time, a different cabbie tried to take me for 30.

'No way,' I said to him, 'it only cost me 20 last time, how can it be 30 now?'

We haggled for a while, even though I knew the bloke was trying to rip me off, and he knew he was trying to rip me off. Eventually I looked at him and said: 'Have you got any children?'

I'm not sure why I asked him that — maybe I was trying to make him feel guilty. At first he was taken aback, but eventually he said he had a couple of kids, and that was when I gave him a 100 dollar bill. Just like that. You should have seen the look on his face. He stared up at me, then looked at the bill, then back at me. It was like a gold bar to him.

'That's cool,' I said. 'You've got two kids, you have the bloody hundred.'

I wonder if his children saw any of it?

Later in the tour, in Georgetown, Guyana, we went to a restaurant for the team dinner before the second Test. The place was called 'The Caribbean Rose'. I remember the dinner well because I sat with manager Lawrie Sawle on one side and coach Bob Simpson on the other, which was unusual. At most team dinners the men in charge — captain, coach, vice-captain, manager — tend to sit together.

It was an enjoyable meal. At that point in the tour everything was going well. We'd won the one-day international series 4–1 and been satisfied with our performance in the drawn first Test. The talk was of positive cricket and, hopefully, a one-nil lead in the series by the time we left Guyana. With dinner over, Lawrie called for the bill, as it is the Australian Cricket Board's habit of paying for these pre-Test dinners.

When Lawrie saw that bill his heart skipped a beat. It came to 29,000 Guyanese dollars! The economy of Guyana wasn't travelling too well at the time (still isn't, I imagine), and with inflation rampant, one Guyanese dollar really was worth less than the paper it was written on. I guess the bill was the equivalent of about 200, maybe 250 Australian dollars.

Our manager didn't have 29,000 Guyanese dollars in cash on him. He reached for the ACB Mastercard. No go, said the Caribbean Rose owner. It had to be cash. How about travellers' cheques? Sorry. Cash!

Things were looking a little embarrassing. Everyone put their hands in their kick, but there was no way we were going to be carrying that sort of cash around — muggings and robberies are a way of life on the streets of Georgetown. International headlines loomed: 'Australian Cricket Team Reneges On Restaurant Bill'. Thoughts of a runner were soon forgotten. Eventually, after much discussion, a compromise was reached and the restaurant owner agreed to hold two signed US$100 travellers' cheques, and in the morning, instead of going to the Test match, Lawrie would head back to The Caribbean Rose and exchange the travellers' cheques for cash.

This compromise led to a scene straight out of a gangster movie. Next morning, as we tucked into breakfast, Lawrie looked like he was setting out to complete a drug deal, as he left the hotel carrying a black briefcase full of notes that stacked up to 29,000 Guyanese dollars. He needed a couple of security guys from our hotel to keep him company along the way.

We felt he should have handcuffed the briefcase to his wrist and kitted him out in sunglasses, dark felt hat and dark suit instead of his Australian blazer and tie, just for added effect.

•CHAPTER 7•

The Prince and the Lord

The West Indies 12th man for each Test of the 1991 series was Brian Lara. It was during the first Test, in Kingston, that I first met the man I call the 'Prince', and it was an introduction I will never forget. Lara was then 21, but looked a lot younger, with his slight frame, teenager's grin and reserved, almost shy, nature. After the first day's play, the West Indies manager, Lance Gibbs, brought the little bloke into the Australian dressing room. While Gibbs mingled around the room, the Prince just stood there, clad in his team blazer and tie, one hand by his side, the other firmly clutching a can of Coke, looking for all the world like the kid who's been invited to the party but doesn't know a soul there.

I had heard of him, of course. We all had — this prodigy who everyone in the Caribbean saw as a potential champion. I was sitting in the corner with Moey Matthews when Gibbs and the Prince walked in. After a while, I jumped up and walked over.

'Brian,' I said and thrust out a hand, 'Mike Whitney. Take your jacket off and come over and have a beer.'

'Thank you. I'm happy with the soft drink,' he replied.

'No problem, come over for a chat.'

Which he did, and Moey, the Prince and I had a long talk. I'll never forget the impression he left on me that day. Later, in

Trinidad, we spent some time together. Everywhere we walked there together, it was: 'Lara! Lara! Lara!' He was incredibly popular, especially considering that at that time he had played just a single Test match. When we tried to enter a nightclub with him, he'd have a quick word with the guy at the door, who'd then look at us and say: 'Matthews and Whitney, no problem, Australian cricket team.' And in we'd go. Without the Prince's blessing, we might never have made it past the front door. It certainly would have cost us plenty to get in.

If that was how he was revered in 1991, I find it hard to even begin to imagine how he is treated today. Then he was a potential star (though I reckon the wise old cricket fans of Trinidad knew he was already a world-beater); now he's the scorer of the highest score in a Test match (375) and first-class match (501 not out).

There's a funny story I can tell about that 501. The Prince scored almost all of those runs on the day the Whitney triplets were born. So it is that one of our daughters is named Madeliene Lara Whitney. Not long after the birth, I took a phone call from a journalist who didn't even know of the babies' arrival, but wanted my reaction to the new world record score.

All I wanted to do was get some sleep, so I just said the first thing that came into my head. 'Why should I be happy about someone doing that?' I mumbled. 'I only got 415 in my whole career. Now he's scored more than that in one bloody day!' That's a joke I've used more than once, in fact it's already appeared a little earlier in this book. But it's a line that was never more appropriate than at that moment. The next thing I did was hang up and the journo never rang back. I guess he was happy with what I had said.

I can't believe what Brian Lara has achieved in cricket. Even if he never scored another run, he'll be a legend of the game because of that three-month period during which he beat the record Test and then the record first-class score. And he's such an unassuming, nice bloke. He's the Michael Slater of West Indian cricket. That's the highest praise I can give the bloke.

Brian Lara wasn't the only 'royalty' we met on that 1991 tour. One day in St Kitts, Merv Hughes and I went for a wander around the ground. The crowd, inevitably, included a great number of young kids, who milled around us. Before long, Merv looked like a cross between Gulliver and the Pied Piper, as a long stream of children buzzed behind his huge frame.

The team we were playing was a President's XI, captained by that brilliant batsman Richie Richardson. In the first innings, we had a bit of luck when Peter Taylor knocked over Richie for just 14, but Keith Arthurton scored 93 and Phil Simmons 71 and the local team reached 332. It was on the second day, while we were batting in our first innings, that Merv and I took our journey around the ground. About halfway around we ran into a little fellow who left us in no doubt whatsoever who his favourite cricketer was.

'Richie RicHARDsaan! Richie RicHARDsaan!! Richie RicHARDsaan!!!' was all he said to us.

Merv could handle that. 'He didn't get too many yesterday,' the big fella chuckled.

I'll never forget the little bloke's reply. The disaster of the first day was obviously long forgotten, as he said: 'If I was Richie RicHARDsaan, I be thinking . . . I was God!'

Merv just looked down at him, I looked at Merv and the kid just sauntered away.

When the President's team batted again, Motor knocked over Richie again, this time for just eight. So when we batted, Merv and I decided to go out and search for our little mate, and when we found him, Merv, grin from ear to ear, couldn't resist.

'Hey, young fella,' Merv shouted out. 'How's God going now?'

It was funny at the time. But when Richie started hammering us all around the Caribbean during the Test series we started thinking that maybe his little fan in St Kitts might not have been too far wide of the mark.

•CHAPTER 8•

Flipper and Fatcat

Two of the finest players in Australian cricket in the early and mid-1980s were Wayne 'Flipper' Phillips and Greg 'Fatcat' Ritchie. Both have now departed from the first-class playing fields, which is a great shame, but I'll always remember them as performers of the highest order and as two of the funniest men I ever toured with. Especially Fatcat — he's just a natural comic.

Both were fantastic players. During his time, Flipper played some of the most amazing innings I have ever seen. Greg Matthews speaks in awe of an innings Wayne played in a Test match in the West Indies, when he smashed the local bowlers — Marshall, Garner, Holding and company — for 120, after coming in at 6–263. Australia finished on 429 that day and Phillips scored 80 of the last 99 runs scored. He was doing crazy things like hammering Garner and Marshall way back over their heads.

Fatcat, too, was an outstanding player. In 1985 he was the second best batsman in the country after AB, having just completed a successful tour of England, on which he scored a century at Trent Bridge and a 94 at Lord's.

Fatcat and Flipper are a potential sensation as a two-man

comedy act. I toured with them to Zimbabwe in 1983, with the Australian under-25 side, and can still picture them at the Harare Sports club on the day they got hold of the ground announcer's microphone and described, in great detail, a succession of major sporting events over the ground's public address system. The match we'd been involved in had ended early on the third day, and I don't think the patrons who lingered after the game ended quite understood what was going on.

It was a beautiful day — not a cloud in the sky and around 30 degrees. We had all showered, changed and congregated on the grass that stretched out onto the field from the Members' stand. That was quite a memorable old structure in itself, and featured some wonderful Dutch architectural touches. We were just relaxing there, more than satisfied after an impressive triumph over the local side and a million miles from home, when over the public address came . . . . 'All set to go in the big one, the Melbourne Cup . . .' We all looked up and there was Fatcat, on the top balcony of the pavilion, microphone in hand . . .

'Kingston Town was first away, with Gurner's Lane and Just a Dash beginning nicely . . .'

When the Cup was finally won, Fatcat handed over to Flipper at the MCG for highlights of the VFL Grand Final. Then it was back to Fatcat, now at Lang Park, to describe a fabulous Wally Lewis try in a State of Origin rugby league match. Then it was a Tony Mundine middleweight championship bout . . .

'A right from Mundine, then a left, a right, a left . . . Monzon's in trouble . . . Mundine's got 'im . . .'

And so it went on for around 20 minutes, as they covered a whole range of Australian sporting events the locals knew very little of, with all called with the verve and aplomb of a professional commentator. It was sensational stuff.

Earlier in the tour Fatcat had had a minor disagreement with our bus driver, a little bloke from Harare who went by the name of Henry, the matter in dispute being who should drive the bus home from a function we had attended. Now that bus was Henry's pride and joy, even though it was owned by one of the firms who were sponsoring the tour. It was some responsibility to look after as well as drive that bus and Henry took his job very seriously indeed.

One evening, after a day's play at the Harare Sports Ground, Cat walked onto the bus and politely asked Henry if he could drive the bus home. Well I must admit he wasn't all that polite. In fact he strode up, grabbed our little bus driver, hoicked him out the door, and planted himself in the driver's seat.

The bus was this poor guy's life. He took that bus home every night. If it got damaged, or stolen, then who knows what his employers would have done.

'Please, Mr Ritchie!' Henry pleaded. 'No, Mr Ritchie, don't drive the bus. Don't drive the bus. Please don't drive the bus'.

And finally: 'I am begging you, Mr Ritchie . . . please, please, please, please do not drive MY bus!'

All Fatcat would say, as he revved the accelerator like Peter Brock on the grid at Bathurst, was: 'I'm driving the bus.' And then he drove the bus home, faster than a speeding bullet, using traffic lights and stop signs as no more than a guide and making sure the bus had a real good look at every side of the road. All the time, Henry just sat there, white, as his bus-driving career flashed before his eyes. I can't begin to tell you how relieved he was when his bus made it safely back to the hotel carpark.

And Fatcat? He just strolled up to his shaking little mate, kissed him on the forehead as he put the keys back in their rightful owner's shirt pocket, and grinned: 'Hey, champ, I like your bus!'

Henry really was a magnificent bloke. When I returned to Zimbabwe in 1986, on a tour with the NSW team, he was still there driving his pride and joy. I loved the guy and many times on that tour we sat together and spoke about his country and about South Africa, and the myriad problems that faced his part

47

of the world. Then in 1987 he was driving the NSW team about again, only by this time his life had changed in a very special way.

'I have some very, very good news for you,' he told me the first time we saw each other on that '87 trip. 'I have had a son!' And then he knocked me over. 'And I have called him Henry . . . Whitney!' He'd named him after the two best blokes in the world according to Henry. At that moment, if Fatcat had wanted to borrow Henry's bus, he'd have had to go through me.

Greg Ritchie would do anything to get a laugh. I've been told about how, on a tour of Pakistan, he terrorised the South Australian cricket writer and former Shield player, Alan 'Sheffield' Shiell. One day Sheffield was sitting by a hotel pool, typing away at a story when Fatcat decided to have some fun. He'd bought some firecrackers, which aren't hard to buy on the sub-continent, and made plans as to how to use them (you can get top-of-the-range stuff — thunders that resemble a stick of dynamite, skyrockets, things that'd get you arrested in Australia — for next to nothing in Pakistan).

Before setting off on his mission, Fatcat, as an added touch, daubed himself in warpaint. He slid along the pool edge, up behind Sheff, and left an almighty firecracker under the journo's chair. Then he slid back, taking with him a two- or three-metre wick he'd made up, so he could light the thing a safe distance from the epicentre. And when this thing went off, Sheff jumped a conservative two metres in the air. The hotel, he quickly concluded in mid-flight, was being bombed. By the time he landed he was whiter than white and a hair's breadth from a heart attack.

But it didn't end there. For the remainder of the tour, whenever there was a dull moment, Fatcat would sneak up behind Sheff . . . and 'hissssss' ever so quietly into his ear. To our intrepid cricket writer that hissing was as loud as a bomb alert in Baghdad and he was forever jumping in the air, and losing another heartbeat whenever Fatcat was around.

One night on tour in Zimbabwe we (the Aussie under-25 team) went to a huge dinner, a very official do at one of Harare's best hotels, and Fatcat took a whoopee cushion with him. The Aussie cricketers were placed two to a table, with the other seats on each table being occupied by a succession of distinguished guests. Fatcat and I were on the same table and not long into the night, he quickly ducked below the tablecloth, blew the cushion up, and then blew his guests away.

'Sorry about that,' he grimaced after the first burst, but soon after he was at it again. I didn't know whether to laugh or cry, while our guests didn't know which way to look, or what to say. 'I'm having a bit of trouble with the local food, folks,' Greg said apologetically, before a succession of short, sharp spurts.

Then, after about 10 minutes, he pulled the thing out, and everyone had a right old laugh.

I think back, and realise such a prank could easily have landed Fatcat in trouble, but he was a naturally funny bloke who has the knack of making people laugh. And I reckon if you have the ability to make people laugh, then you're going to end with a truckload of friends.

•CHAPTER 9•

Calling Dr Jones

When we stayed in St Kitts, our first stop on the '91 tour of the West Indies, we really were given a magic place to commence a cricket tour. Or any tour for that matter. We were able to enjoy a marvellous panoramic view, accommodated in bungalows located right on the beach, no more than 15 metres from the sand.

Straight after our first team practice I charged down to check out the surf. The beach was sensational and the waves were a fairly good size, but very hollow. And pounding.

I was the only one who ventured into the water, not so much because no one else was game, but because the other guys decided they'd rather be sleeping off the last remnants of our long flight to the Caribbean. However, not long after I hit the water, I looked back to shore and saw Dean Jones standing on the beach, all on his own. With the bungalows camouflaged by the trees lining the sand, he looked like a modern-day Robinson Crusoe standing there alone on his island.

Deano was watching me, and he must have been thinking: 'This looks all right . . . if a bit heavy.' It wasn't a big surf, but there were more than a few really nasty dumpers and a bit of an undertow. Even so, I was having a great time, bodysurfing a few tubes, and Deano's the sort of guy who'll back himself at everything. He's a very good sportsman, so it doesn't matter if he's on the golf course, the tennis court, training ground, anywhere — he thinks he's a chance. And he hates losing. That's just Dean Jones, and his attitude and approach radiates from him whenever he turns to sport.

He decided to join me, but about 15 minutes later, after the sea was finished with him, he must have eaten at least three tonnes of sand. I'd say: 'No, Deano, when you take off just put your arm out straight and try and go across the face of the wave.' So he'd do something like what I had explained, and bang . . . he would be down again.

Later in the tour, when we arrived in Barbados, I did exactly as I had done in St Kitts — checked out the beach. It was all good news, a real picture-postcard location, beautiful clear blue water, and some pretty shapely three to four footers breaking not too far from shore. A few of us who had grown up near the water were out there in no time, having the time of our lives. The conditions were great and we were bodysurfing these barrels like there was no tomorrow. It was fantastic and soon most of the guys were trying their luck.

For a while Deano stayed on the beach, as if the memory of St Kitts was checking him, but eventually he decided to have another go. Now the waves were really sucking up. It was basically a take-off, then the two-second tube, and then duck under and swim out the back of the wave. There is a bit of technique involved in this sort of thing — stay in the wave too long and you risk a headache.

I hoped Deano might have improved since St Kitts but, no, he got hammered again . . . and again . . . and again. And then hammered some more. A wave would build up, Deano would start swimming . . . and then, bang, in a mist of spray and white water, down he would go. And then he'd come up, coughing and spluttering, and we'd think: 'Why the hell is he letting this happen to him?'

DEAN JONES GOES BODY SURFING

He just wouldn't give up. Nothing, not even Mother Nature, was going to stop him from being at least a reasonable body-surfer. His competitive spirit was such that there was no way he was getting out of there until he'd proven to himself and his mates that he could handle what the ocean was throwing at him.

He'd swim out again and again, and mutter to us: 'Shit, this is a big surf.' It was only a three footer, but to Deano it was Pipeline. He looked like a drowned rat.

A lot of people know Deano as 'Lege', as in legend. He'll even call himself that from time to time. I remember Greg Matthews one day walking up to him during a Shield match and saying: 'There's only one legend and it ain't you. It's Doug Walters.'

After that Greg just turned and walked away. I'm not quite sure what Deano made of it.

53

A very competitive man. And a bloke who, in his own eyes, has never done anything wrong. In Jamaica in 1991 we were roomies. I arrived home there one afternoon, and there was a security guard at our hotel room door. 'Well, Mr Whitney,' he says, 'you've gone out and left the door open . . .'

We'd had a net in the morning, and then come back to the hotel. 'When I left around midday,' I told the guard, 'Mr Jones was asleep.'

'Well, Mr Jones is not around and the door was left open.'

I went into the room, checked a few things and then realised my precious camera was gone. Stolen. I couldn't believe it. I'd had that camera since 1981, it had been round the world with me, to Africa, Asia, America, Europe. About 50 countries in all. It was a fully-manual camera that I loved using — none of this automatic business for me. I must have taken 10,000 photographs with it. Now it was gone.

My heart just sank. It was like a part of me had been knocked off. And what distressed me even more was that this was possibly the one and only fair dinkum Australian cricket tour I was ever going to be on. The opportunity to document it fully and faithfully on celluloid had been taken away. Already we'd been in St Kitts and Jamaica, with so many other exciting adventures still to come. It was like my left arm had been taken. As all these thoughts began to multiply in my mind you can imagine how I was feeling.

I waited for Dean to return. When he did I confronted him. 'Deano,' I said, 'you left the bloody door open!'

'Who did?' he replied.

'You did!'

'No, I didn't.'

'Well, who did? I've arrived home and there's a security guy on the door. When I left, you were asleep on the bed. I couldn't have left the door open. If you didn't leave it open, who did?'

'I don't know.'

And then, after a while, he added: 'Oh . . . maybe it didn't slam shut properly.'

He's an amazing guy and a great batsman, who has played some of the best digs I've ever seen. Sometimes, though, I've been dumbfounded by the amount of luck he's had. In Sri Lanka in 1992 he scored a Test century, in the second innings of the second Test, but was dropped by the keeper when he was five, should have been stumped when he was 10, was dropped in the slips at 25, and offered at least another two chances before he reached three figures. Once Deano charged down the wicket, missed, and turned around to see the keeper grab the ball, miss the stumps as he tried to complete the stumping, and then drop the ball as he tried to swing back and hit the bails at the second attempt. Deano was the best part of three metres out — he just strolled back and put his bat down while the keeper pounded the ground in despair. While all this was going on, Mark Waugh was just shaking his head in the dressing room. In the same game he had to wear a 'pair', the first duck after first slip took a spectacular catch, the second after he copped a red-hot lbw decision.

That knock in Sri Lanka came a full decade after I first saw Dean Jones on the cricket field. In his first Shield match against NSW he produced a stunning display. Henry hit him right in the gob not long after he walked out to bat in Victoria's second innings. It was an ugly blow and Dean went down. But then he got up again, and batted on to get 94. From that moment on, as far as we Blues were concerned, Deano's courage was never in question.

A season later, he was on the plane to Zimbabwe with the Australian under-25 team — the youngest bloke in the squad. At one point late in that tour, while the team was playing in Bulawayo, Fatcat Ritchie developed a very ugly cyst on a very ugly part of the body. I will never forget the screams I heard one day from an adjoining room in our hotel at that time. My roomie, Rod McCurdy, dashed out to find out what was causing all the commotion and returned with the news that Fatcat was sitting on the toilet in his room in a great deal of pain. He clearly had a problem, which turned out to be serious enough for Greg to be airlifted back to Harare for the cyst to be cut off the end of his bowel.

The surgery left an awful wound that couldn't be stitched and consequently required a change of dressing every single day. Given the location of the problem there was no earthly way Fatcat could make the alterations himself; instead he was given the opportunity to select an unfortunate soul who would have to change the dressing for him.

Every day Fatcat chose the youngest member of the squad — Deano.

I will never forget Greg sitting up on the dressing room table, clean dressing by his side, legs wide apart, announcing in that voice you hear in hospitals all round the world:

'Dr Jones, Dr Jones . . . wanted in surgery . . . Dr Jones.'

And all Deano could do was report for duty, to complete this hideous job. But he did it every day. And as far as I knew Fatcat was more than pleased with the job Dr Jones carried out.

As I explained, there's absolutely *nothing* Dean Jones won't try and do as well as he possibly can.

•CHAPTER 10•

Australia's Pocket Hercules

I first ran into David Boon, the man Billy Birmingham called 'the five foot two Tasmanian with the flared pants', during my debut season in first-class cricket — 1980–81 — when he was playing for Tasmania. Then, when I went to England in 1981, we were rival pros in the Northern League. When we played against each other during that Australian winter, I knocked him over in one game, and he scored a heap of runs in the other. And ever since we've been good mates. In 1983, we were together again, on the Australian under-25 team's tour of Zimbabwe.

Boonie is special in his own way. You rarely see him out on the town, instead he'll be found in a quiet spot at the hotel bar with one or two of his team-mates. He'll see some of his colleagues heading out for the evening, but rarely join them. 'Where you goin'?' he'll say. 'To the such-and-such Italian restaurant down the road. You want to join us?' Almost always Boonie would knock the invitation back, preferring his two or three beers at the bar, after which he'd be off to his room . . . to hit the pillow. Next day he'll be out at the ground, scoring runs.

It's not that he never goes out or never has a good time. He sure does. But the quiet approach is his way. Dare I say it, the

Tasmanian way. And it sure works. A lot of the time you never know he's there — he's not the type of guy to take over a team meeting or run around the ground in celebration. A lot of people who don't know better bag him on the score of his tubby physique, but he's a fit, strong boy. Real hard. You touch him anywhere — even his gut — and he's as solid as a rock. And he's one of these guys who never complains about injuries and setbacks. His character is as tough as his physique.

Over the past few years he's suffered from a succession of knee injuries, but, apart from the odd occasion when he's had to drop out of a less-important game, the public would never know about it.

One day, Boonie talked me through the training program he sets himself to stay on the paddock. It's unbelievable! I was calling him 'Hercules' by the end of the conversation. 'Hey, Herc,' I'd yell out. 'How's the 3000 leg-raises going?'

If someone came up to me when I was working my way back from one of my knee operations, to ask how the rehabilitation was going, I'd say: 'Mate, it's a battle. I'm working my arse out. All those bloody stretches, and leg lifts, and the bike, and the swimming. It's cruel.'

But not Boonie. From him you'd get no more than: 'Oh, it's going okay.'

David Boon has been the Australian team's short leg for longer than most of us can remember. As well as being one of the greatest close-in men of them all, he'd have to be the most undemonstrative short-leg fieldsman in history. In contrast, whenever I took a wicket for NSW, Jack Small would be racing up from in close to give me a big, big bear hug. But if I took a wicket for Australia, Boonie's celebration would amount to no more than a slap on the shoulder as I raced through. But that's not to say that Boonie was not as happy as Jack. Far from it. In its own way his slap on the shoulder had just as much feeling and excitement as Jack's rugby tackle. And it was

something I appreciated — recognition from a very dedicated and very successful professional.

I remember going into the Aussie dressing room during the sixth Test, at The Oval, of the 1993 tour of England. Australia were just about to begin their first innings after England had been dismissed early on the second day, and Mark Taylor and Michael Slater were doing their final stretches before heading out to the middle. Meanwhile, Boonie was sitting on the dressing-room bench, wearing nothing more than a jock-strap, with all his gear laid out neatly around him. In his right hand was a freshly lit cigarette. He loves a fag, Boonie, eats them. In his left was a can of Diet Coke. When I saw the drink I thought: 'At least he's watching his weight.'

During that Test series, Boonie scored centuries in the second, third and fourth Tests, and 93 in the first Test, at Old Trafford. No Australian had scored hundreds in three successive Tests in England since the legend himself, DG Bradman, in 1938. By the end of that Ashes series, a real good case could have been put together for David Boon being the most effective run-scorer in the game. Whether he was better than Richardson and Crowe, Mark Waugh and Javed Miandad, I wasn't sure. But he might have been.

As I looked at Boonie in The Oval dressing room that day, at his cigarette, his soft drink and his dress sense I realised I was not looking at a pretty sight. And I day-dreamed a scene in my mind. Suddenly, through the dressing-room door came some of the world's other great sporting champions — Carl Lewis, Michael Jordan, Kieren Perkins, Pete Sampras — and it was my job to explain to these out-and-out superstars what cricket was all about.

And when I finished my quick exposé of the sport, I pointed over to the dressing-room corner and added: 'And, by the way, that little guy in the jock strap over there . . . he's the best batsman in the world.'

And then I tried to imagine the looks on their faces.

•CHAPTER 11•

Mark Waugh: Something to Bet On

For all Mark Waugh's runs, and his many brilliant innings, I know we are still to see the best of him in Test cricket. The reason I'm so confident about this relates to some of the things I saw him do for NSW while we were team-mates. Pure and simple, Mark Waugh was the best player I played with or against in first-class cricket. I was very lucky in my time to play against so many of the post-War legends — Gavaskar, Greg Chappell, Viv, Javed Miandad, AB — but I rate Mark at the very top of the list.

You may think me mad for saying that, and I realise his Test-career batting average doesn't support such a rating, but I honestly believe he's *that* good.

For much of his career he's had to suffer a view held by many people that he doesn't value his wicket enough. I had a long talk with him once, about this perception people have of him as a lazy cricketer, and suggested that it was this apparent laziness that has stopped him being recognised as a champion. He replied: 'Roy, that really annoys me. I'm not lazy — it's just the way I play. Do you really think that I want to get out?'

Junior usually doesn't say a lot on the cricket field, but I remember a Test against India in Adelaide in early 1992, when one of the umpires gave a caught behind decision against us, a ruling we didn't agree with. At the next change of overs, Mark walked over to the ump and sneered: 'What? Is there one rule for them, and another for us . . .'

And then he gave the ump a gobful.

I couldn't believe it. It was so out of character for Junior to let fly with an outburst like that. I went up to him and said: 'Mate, don't forget you've got to bat with this ump in this game, for the rest of the season, and for the rest of your career.'

Later in the same match, Mark went out to bat and straightaway the inevitable happened. One jagged, went between bat and pad, caught the inside of his back leg and finished up with the keeper. The Indians appealed, more out of hope than anything, but Mark was given out by, of course, the same umpire. Now, I'm not suggesting that the ump gave the decision in any

way other than the way he saw it, but his verdict shattered poor Junior, who was in something of a slump and fighting to keep his spot in the team. I don't think I've ever seen a bloke walk so slowly off the Adelaide Oval. He sort of stumbled up the steps, fumbling with his batting gloves, and then sat on the dressing-room bench, staring at the floor, totally dejected.

I knew what he was going through, but I couldn't resist. I just poked my head around the corner, and whispered ever so quietly: 'Told ya.'

He looked up at me and suggested that that hadn't been the right thing to say. But, though he may not have agreed with me just at that moment, I think he learned a very valuable lesson.

He loves a bet does M. Waugh. There's a TV in the dressing room at the SCG, and it's forever on SKY Channel, the horse-racing network, because Junior always wants to watch the races. No-one else gets a choice. One day, he was out in the middle scoring another Shield century, and a few of us decided to change the channel, at least until he was dismissed. I grabbed the remote control and hit the channel selector button to see what else was on. First button . . . SKY Channel. Next button . . . SKY Channel. Then . . . SKY Channel. SKY Channel. SKY Channel. He'd locked every bloody button on SKY! There was no way he was going to take the chance of missing a race because someone else was watching something else.

He knows racing form backwards and has probably seen as many racetracks in his time as he's seen cricket grounds. He's been to the races in England, Sri Lanka, the West Indies, everywhere. If we were ever interstate, say Brisbane, and he had the chance, he was out to Doomben or Eagle Farm. He knows their colours, training, breeding, star signs, good and bad habits. I don't know how he has time to squeeze in cricket.

I recall that when he got out for his fourth Test duck in succession in Sri Lanka in 1992, he just couldn't believe it. He was just sitting there, blank faced. His whole world had caved in. He looked terrible and I took it upon myself to try and cheer him up. I didn't have a clue how, after all, he'd just been through a run drought not even the world's worst tailender had surely ever had to endure. All I could say was: 'Gee, I wish I could have got a bit of money on Mark Waugh getting four globes in a row in Test cricket.'

And he looked up, and just the barest grin formed on the corner of his mouth.

'Hell, Roy,' he said. 'We could have made a fortune!'

•CHAPTER 12•

How Good Was Dougie?

Not long back, at the launch of the NSW Blues 1994–95 season, I had a brief chat with one of the legends of the game, Neil Harvey. During the function, which was held in a marquee on the SCG, the NSW team came out and ran around the ground, going through a series of exercises and fielding drills. I noticed Neil gazing out to where the Blues were doing some stretches, and then he turned to me and said: 'We never did that sort of thing in my day.'

I couldn't let it go. 'Neil,' I said with a wink to the other blokes in our group, 'can you imagine how much better a player you would have been if you had done all of that stuff?'

He just turned around and looked at me with a quizzical look on his face. Then he looked back at the cricketers running their laps, took a sip from his wine glass . . . and shook his head.

He never said a word. Didn't need to.

Neil Harvey would undoubtedly enjoy a story I tell from time to time. It's a yarn that revolves around one of my first sporting heroes, the legendary Doug Walters, and was passed on to me by Kerry O'Keeffe, a great bloke who goes by the nickname of 'Skull'. Kerry, of course, played many times for

NSW, and 24 times in Tests for Australia between 1970 and 1977.

As anyone with any knowledge of cricket folklore knows, Dougie loves a smoke, a beer and a late night. In his playing days he also loved to have people sharing these vices with him (or at least the latter two) which was always fine for Dougie, but not quite so for his team-mates who had to bat or bowl the following day. Or, as was often the case, bat or bowl later that *morning*.

As I related in my book *Quick Whit*, Dougie got me on the night that immediately followed my first day in first-class cricket. Our captain, Rick McCosker, had warned me to be 'wary of Doug', but, what the heck, Dougie was my hero, so when the invitation came from the Great One for a night out on the town I jumped at the chance. A few hours and many drinks later, while Dougie appeared as steady and chirpy as ever, I was a complete mess.

Kerry's story concerns a Test match between Australia and New Zealand that was played at Lancaster Park in Christchurch in early 1977. The track was a bit green when the match began, and Kiwi captain Glenn Turner sent the Aussies in to bat. By the time Dougie came in, the Australians were struggling a bit at 4–112, but he proceeded to play one of his finest hands, and by stumps was 129 not out. At the other end for most of Walters' masterpiece was another renowned party-goer, Gary 'Gus' Gilmour, who by stumps was unbeaten on 65. He'd come to the wicket at 6–208, and by close of play the pair had added 137 for the seventh wicket.

Kerry O'Keeffe was down in the scorebook as the next man in. He was well aware that if one of either Walters or Gilmour fell the next morning, he would be required to play an important innings. The chance was there to build a huge first-innings total and squeeze the Kiwis right out of the Test. There was no way he was going to let himself, his captain, his team-mates or his country down, so he made plans for a quiet evening in the hotel bistro and an early night.

For quite a time things went according to plan. By 11pm, Kerry's head was on the pillow and not even the stress of playing in a Test match stopped him from drifting straight off to sleep. But at some very ugly ensuing hour of the morning he was woken by a commotion in the corridor outside his room, followed by a loud banging on his door. Kerry's first response was to roll over, clasp the pillow tightly around his head, and try to get back to sleep. But the knocking was too persistent and eventually he had to get up and see what was going on.

It was the two not out batsmen, just back from a night roaming the bars of Christchurch.

'C'mon, Skull,' he heard from behind the closed door, 'we know you're in there. Why don't you come out for a drink with your mates?'

Now Kerry was a bloke who usually didn't mind a quiet drink. But now he had his country to think of. With the latch and chain firmly in place, he opened the door just a little, and looked at his two happy colleagues.

'Listen, you bastards,' he whispered. 'You're all right. You've got your runs. But I'm the bloke that's going to have to go in tomorrow at one minute past 11 after one of you gets out, so get lost and leave me alone.'

'C'mon, Skull,' they cried in unison, 'don't let us down!'

Eventually, they went on their way and Kerry went back to his bed, to try and rescue the sleep he'd lost. Fortunately, the next morning, he felt okay which was more than could be said for his comrades. On the bus that took them to the ground, as captain Greg Chappell ran through plans for the day, the two not out batsmen slept through the entire trip. At the ground, while most of the side set off on a few warm-up laps, Dougie and Gus preferred to stay in the dressing room to prepare for their innings. On his way to the middle, Gus stumbled and dropped his bat, and, as the pair played and missed during the

first few overs, Kerry went through his stretching routine, fully aware that at any second he would be required in the middle.

Or so he thought . . .

After about half an hour, Dougie reached his 150. Then it was announced that a new seventh-wicket Australian partnership record had been established, breaking the old record held by Rod Marsh and . . . Kerry O'Keeffe. Then came the 200 stand (in just 165 minutes, the second 100 in just 71), then the first century of Gary Gilmour's Test career.

It was ridiculous. Here were two men, who by all rights should have been struggling to see the ball, carving up an attack that included, among others, Richard Hadlee. Finally, when the stand reached 217, Gus edged one from Ewen Chatfield back onto his stumps, bringing Kerry at last out to the middle.

To make the story perfect, Kerry should have been dismissed first ball for a duck, and that's the way I usually tell it when I'm speaking at a function. The truth is not quite that amusing, but it's close. In fact, Kerry was dropped when he was nought, by the keeper Warren Lees, but ended up making eight before he was run out after calling for a quick leg-bye. I often wonder if Dougie might have run him out on purpose, as a get-square. Why the hell Kerry O'Keeffe was calling for a quick leg-bye when his partner had been up to 4am is totally beyond me — I guess you'll have to ask Kerry about that.

What is definitely true is Dougie's reaction after the run out. As you can imagine, Kerry was not too pleased to get only eight after spending the night in his hotel room — when his mates had both scored hundreds (in Doug's case, 250) after spending the night on the town. In fact, not too pleased is a rather large understatement. He was totally pissed off. And the look on Dougie's face as Kerry walked off didn't help either. It was very clear that Dougie was having a lot of trouble not laughing. By the time Kerry walked past Dougie on the way back to the pavilion, the Great Man could contain himself no longer.

He didn't say anything — didn't need to — he just waited until Kerry was alongside . . . and then, quietly but oh so effectively, he started to chuckle.

•CHAPTER 13•

He Who Laughs Last

I reckon the best way to judge the quality of a practical joke is by how much laughter you get out of it, and whether the guy on the receiving end can see the funny side of it as well.

At the time I was selected in the Australian team for the fifth Test against the Windies, in Adelaide in 1989, most of the guys had organised for their kits to be transferred straight from Sydney (where the fourth Test had been played) to Adelaide. This created quite a problem for Tim May. The bags were waiting for the guys in the Adelaide Oval dressing room, and when we walked into the room there was something of a stench in the air, which seemed to be coming from Maysie's bag. With a great deal of trepidation, he opened up his kit setting off an ugly chain reaction. The inside of the bag *stank . . .* really stank. Half of us had to race out of the room. One or two all but vomited.

It turned out Steve Waugh had stuffed Maysie's boots and gloves with prawn heads before the bags left Sydney. I'll leave it to your imagination to figure out what that did to the contents of the kit.

That was one joke that worked really well, but if you're judging them on laughs, it didn't rate that highly. Most of us felt too crook to laugh at the time, though we did have a quiet chuckle a little later on. Whether Maysie has ever forgiven him, I'm not really sure. I bet he's never forgotten, though.

One of the favourite jokes was played time and again during my season of league cricket in 1983, and reached the stage where our batsmen were afraid to put their jockstraps on. The idea was to douse the jockstraps in Dencorub, which is a product that, if put on in too large a quantity, can burn . . . and burn . . . and burn.

However, it can take a little while to have an impact. The ideal situation was for a wicket to fall quickly, so a batsman would be on his way to the middle before he felt the first stirrings of this horrendous burning sensation. The opposition and spectators wouldn't have a clue what was going on, as the

incoming batsman rubbed feverishly at his groin and was for-ever stopping to adjust his protector.

Many a time the next man in would be sitting on a chair, waiting for a wicket to fall, when he'd suddenly leap to his feet and say: 'You fookin' bastards! . . .'

One day in Zimbabwe in 1983, the entire Australian under-25 team was at Bulawayo airport, the morning after a victory celebration, waiting for a flight back to Harare. Our fast bowler, Rod McCurdy, had celebrated as hard as anyone, and was crashed out on an airport lounge. Unfortunately, he had made the mistake of lying down directly under an overhead balcony. From that balcony, Greg Ritchie slowly lowered a huge plastic spider, which he'd tied to a long piece of string.

Fatcat edged the spider down very gradually, and in doing so created a wonderful air of tension. One person would notice it, then another and another. By the time the spider reached Rod, the whole airport was aware of what was going on and waited for our paceman's reaction.

He shit himself! 'AAARRRGGGHHH!!!' he roared, while the entire airport terminal laughed ourselves silly. Fatcat broke up completely and I think maybe even Rod appreciated the joke a few hours later when he calmed down.

The honour of having played the funniest practical joke I ever saw during my cricket career must go to one of NSW's finest ever fast bowlers, the great Len Pascoe. One day in Newcastle, early in my career with the Blues, Lennie decided it was time to have some fun. Being a bit short of ideas he eventually settled on the old 'bowl of water on top of the slightly opened door so that the next bloke who walks through gets totally drenched' trick.

With great precision he set everything up but, sadly, about 20 minutes went by and not one person walked through the door. Lennie, who had been sitting on one of the dressing room benches eagerly waiting to see who he would embarrass, couldn't believe that no-one had been caught and eventually grew sick of waiting. He departed by another door, leaving the bowl up where he had put it.

'Hey, guys,' he said as he was leaving, 'let me know how the bowl of water joke goes.'

There was a group of us there playing cards. 'Okay, Lennie,' we said, 'not a problem.'

Another half hour went by. By this stage we'd all forgotten the bowl was there. Then, suddenly there was a great commotion. Someone had stormed through the door, and Lennie's water had crashed down, leaving the unfortunate bloke all but drowned and with a nasty lump on his head where the bowl had landed.

And who was that unfortunate person?

Lennie Pascoe!!

• CHAPTER 14 •

What Happens on the Field, Stays on the Field

Some of the things grade cricketers get up to can be quite bizarre. I once heard about a bloke who opened the batting for Mosman in the Sydney first-grade competition and superglued sandpaper onto the face of his bat, because his job was to take the shine off the new ball.

However, of all the cricketers I played against in Sydney grade cricket, a fellow called Brian Riley was the craziest. I first heard his name mentioned in my first season of first grade, with Randwick back in 1979–80. One of my more senior team-mates pulled me aside one day and said quietly: 'You won't really have an idea of how hard the top grade can be until we play Petersham. They're captained by Brian Riley.'

It was the way he said 'Brian Riley' that stayed with me. It was muttered in much the same way I imagine the name 'Attila the Hun' was whispered throughout Europe during the 5th century. Riley, I was informed, was a captain who played the game of cricket extremely hard, with no sixteenth asked or given.

'What's he like as a bloke?' I asked.

'He's a bit loopy,' was the reply. 'He'll try and bait you. Just don't listen to him.'

A few weeks later the clash arrived. Randwick versus Petersham, at Petersham Oval. They batted first, a couple of wickets fell to M. Whitney, and he was in. Brian Riley. It had to be a bumper first ball, and it was, fired in with all the youthful strength and vigour I could muster. And what did Brian Riley do? No problem, he just stepped inside the line and hooked me for four, backward of square. And then he walked down the wicket, stared straight at me and said, in a voice just loud enough for everyone in the ground to hear: 'Keep bowlin' 'em there . . . sonny.'

Sonny!! I couldn't believe it. What right did this old prick have to call me anything like that? The next bouncer was even quicker and aimed right at the Petersham emblem on his cap, but Brian Riley just grinned and leaned out of the way. 'Is that your best . . . BOY?' he laughed down the wicket. For the rest of that over, and until I was hauled out of the attack without taking another wicket, I tried my best to kill him. Not to get him out . . . that would have been too good for him. I was thinking homicide. However, as I stewed at fine leg after the last over of my spell, I began to realise that not only could he talk, Brian Riley could play a bit as well.

Not that any of that really mattered. I still hated him.

At tea, in our dressing room, I copped a terrible hiding from my own team-mates. 'What about that Brian Riley,' they giggled as one. 'He sure made you look silly . . . sonny.'

By stumps, still without another wicket, I was an angry young man. I changed in a hurry — I had to get out of there — but our skipper, Alan Turner, insisted we stay for a beer or two with our opponents. So the two sides mingled, and I decided that if the bastard said just one word to me, I was going to belt him. He was sitting over in the corner of the Petes' dressing room, so I stayed as far away from that location as possible. But then he was striding through the pack towards me. I clenched my fist, and waited for the trigger. But instead of another jibe he shot his right hand out, complete with a cold tinnie, and asked: 'Want a beer, mate?'

I looked at the can and the smile on his face, and learned a lesson right there and then. 'I thought you bowled well early on today, son,' he said to me, and I could tell he really meant it. We talked for a little while, and I began to realise Brian Riley was a real good bloke, if a real bastard on the cricket field.

What happens on the field, stays on the field. It's one of the oldest adages in the game, and one of the most important.

A few years later, when he was winding down his career in the lower grades, he'd still make his way to Petersham Oval for the first hour of first grade, just so he could have an impact on the play. I remember him sitting up there on the hill and shouting a gobful of abuse at John Dyson, who was opening the batting for us. 'How the bloody hell did you ever make first grade, Dyson?' Brian was screaming at the top of his voice, in the hope he'd goad the Test man into trying an inappropriate shot. 'You're the biggest imposter in the history of cricket.' The tirade wouldn't stop until it was time for Brian to set off for his own game.

Brian will never change. Even today, I can be walking past the tennis courts located between the SCG and the Sydney Football Stadium and a fight will break out between four elderly gentlemen playing doubles.

'How the bloody hell can that be out?' one of the four will be yelling above the rest. 'You can't be serious!!!'

That's Brian Riley.

•CHAPTER 15•

Lillee and Thommo

When I first made the Australian team in 1981, I was very humbled just to be in the same team as world record holders like DK Lillee and Rod Marsh. One day these guys were idols . . . the next they were team-mates. The players who had done so much to get Australian cricket to the very top of the tree in the mid-1970s — famous names such as Lillee, Marsh, Greg Chappell, Ian Chappell, Walters and Thomson — had a real aura about them, and at that time I considered myself very privileged to even be on first-name terms with some of them.

It seems to have changed a bit now. I see young blokes, new to the Sheffield Shield, walking up to David Boon and saying: 'Howzit goin', Babs?'

Babs!!!

They've played maybe one season of first-class cricket while Boonie's been a legend for at least a decade. Until David says otherwise, I reckon it should definitely be 'Mr Boon'.

Or 'Sir'.

The first time I found myself on the same cricket field as Dennis Lillee was in a NSW v Western Australia Shield match at the WACA in Perth in 1980–81. Matches between the Blues and the Sandgropers were as hard in those days as they are

79

today. Which means HARD. I was 12th man for the Blues. During the NSW first innings, Lillee hit our keeper/batsman Steve 'Stumper' Rixon on the chin with a bouncer. Stumper was wearing a helmet without a face-guard and the ball cannoned into the 'chin-cap' which was part of the strap that kept the helmet on his head.

Stumper didn't go down — he's a tough man — but did call for some assistance from the dressing room. There was a trickle of blood, so medico Mike Whitney raced out with a towel, a glass, a jug of water and the best of intentions. By the time I reached the centre a couple of West Australians — both umpires — were looking after Steve. He took the towel, wiped away the blood and then poured himself a drink. He was a little shaken but otherwise okay.

Without warning, we were interrupted by Lillee, who snatched the jug from me . . . and drank the lot. He looked like the bloke from the *Solo* TV commercial, with half the drink going down his throat and the rest pouring over his chin and shirt. It didn't seem right — here was all this water, which was suppose to be saving the batsman's life, dripping down the moustache of the bloke who'd caused the damage. Lillee handed the empty jug back to me (I said 'thank you'), glared at Stumper and then turned abruptly and strode back to his bowling mark.

I don't know what sort of impact he had on Steve (he ended up getting 50), but I know I was shitting myself!

One day during my second Test match, at the Oval in 1981, I was fielding at mid-off while Dennis was in the middle of a long spell. After a ball had been allowed to go through to Rod Marsh, it was transferred, via second slip, gully and cover to me. This was all fine, except at that point of my career I was the world's worst under-armer. I reckon that if I had been the guy Greg Chappell had asked to bowl that infamous underarm delivery to New Zealand's Brian McKechnie at the conclusion of that one-day international at the MCG earlier that year — the one that caused such a furore on both sides of the Tasman

— I would have said: 'No way, Greg, it's not worth the risk. We'll lose if I underarm six wides in a row.'

My situation at The Oval was one of the great pressure points of my career. Here was the legendary DK Lillee walking back to his mark, sweat pouring from him, with his arm outstretched waiting for the ball. I lobbed it towards him . . . and it didn't miss by much. I reckon he might even have been able to reach it if he'd jumped up maybe a fraction. But not DK. He just left his arm where it was and kept walking back to his mark. He did, though, turn his head ever so slightly so he could watch the ball sail off towards the mid-wicket boundary.

There was nothing I could do but chase the bloody thing. It was a simple case of the old master saying to the young bull: 'Hey, you, throw it HERE! Not *around about* here.' By the time I finally reached the ball, about 20 metres inside the boundary, I was copping a good old razz from the crowd. I picked the ball up and quickly ran back towards my fielding position, stopping on the way to hand the ball back to the bowler.

Despite that experience, I will always love the man and the way he enjoys life. DK Lillee is always full of spirit and life. I have never once run into Dennis in the years since we shared a hotel room in Manchester in 1981 when he hasn't rapped me on the shoulder and said something like: 'G'day, Whits, howzit goin'? How's your mum, the legendary Mrs Whit?'

He's almost always on a high. One of the rare occasions when I saw him just a little below par occurred during the 1993 Australian tour of England, when I was commentating for Channel Nine. Dennis was over there on a type of working holiday — promotional work, coaching, public speaking and calling the cricket — and had asked his father, Keith, to go along with him.

One morning at the cricket, I saw Keith struggling to get up a flight of stairs. 'Gee, Keith,' I said, 'you look a bit crook.'

'That bloody young bloke of mine,' he replied. 'He's never changed. He always loves a night out . . .'

Not long after, I saw Dennis having similar trouble with the same flight of stairs.

'What's the trouble, Master?' I asked him. 'Have a late night?'

'I've felt better,' he answered in a croaky voice. 'It's that old man of mine. He never wants to go home.'

DK Lillee's most famous partner was, of course, Jeff Thomson. My most vivid memory of facing Thommo's bowling came at just about the end of his great career, during a NSW v Queensland Shield match at the SCG in 1985–86. As usual I was batting at number 11, and my comrade at the batting crease was a guy called Wayne Mulherin, a spinner making his first-class debut, who was batting at number 9. When I came out, Wayne was yet to score his first run.

As I had made my first-class debut more than five years earlier, I was very much the senior partner, a point Wayne was quick to concede. Before I took guard, we had a quick mid-pitch conference.

'What's the plan, Michael?' he asked me.

'You can call me Whit,' I said, before outlining my strategy. 'I tell you what . . . if Thommo pitches the ball up, I'm swinging as hard as I can.'

And then we went back to our respective ends.

Sure enough, Thommo went for the yorker, but it ended up a half-volley and somehow I hit it okay. It went back past him and all the way to the fence for four.

'Shit, you hit that one all right,' gasped Wayne. 'How did you know he was going to pitch it there?'

'It's cool,' I whispered back. I didn't want Thommo hearing any of this.

The next one pitched on just about the same spot, but was about four yards quicker and kicked up towards my ribs. I threw my head back and somehow bunted it off beyond the

short legs and out towards the square-leg umpire for an easy single. The fact I was still alive made me feel pretty good. The single was a bonus.

As I reached the other end, the umpire called 'over' and I saw Thommo snatch his hat and storm off towards fine leg. I turned and headed down for another mid-pitch discussion. When I got there and before I could say anything, Wayne knocked me over:

'Gee, Michael, you're counting the number of balls as well!' he exclaimed.

In all my years of cricket that was one tactic that had *never* occurred to me.

•CHAPTER 16•

Up Periscope

In Ian Botham's book on the 1981 England v Australia Test series, *The Incredible Tests 1981*, he wrote of the final stages of Australia's second innings in the Fifth Test, at Old Trafford . . .

'Alderman was no problem. We fancied taking his wicket any time. We also fancied a quick dismissal of Whitney if he was batting behind Alderman . . .'

That's a pretty big sledge on 'Clem' Alderman's batting prowess and I got the hint, reading between the lines, that Both wasn't all that keen on my ability with the willow either. However, in the first innings of that fifth Test, I'd batted ahead of Clem, and there's a bit of a story behind that . . .

As is well documented, I had been playing that season with the Fleetwood club in the north of England. The league matches there were always played on weekends, but there were a number of friendly games scheduled for during the week, and if I wasn't involved elsewhere, I was always happy to play in such matches. Even though they were called 'friendlies', the games were very competitive, and it was usually not until the after-match drinks that the real reason they were considered social became apparent.

It was not rare for teams to organise 10-day tours, in which they'd play seven or eight of these matches in different parts of the country. Just about every day they'd be playing cricket — in Yorkshire, Lancashire, the Lakes district, Scotland, wherever — and every night the boys would be on the sherbet. It's a crazy concept, hard on the body . . . and fantastic.

On one particular Wednesday in Fleetwood, the Redditch Cricket Club arrived in town for a 'friendly'. A couple of my Aussie mates were also in Fleetwood, so our side for the contest had a real Oz flavour about it. I was keen to impress my mates, so I pleaded with our captain, Harold Wilkinson, for the chance to open the batting — something I'd never done all year.

'You've never given me a go,' I told him. 'Just let me open up this once and we'll see how I go.'

Finally he said okay. My opening partner was Peter Rainer, who we called 'Wanta', after the great Cuban athlete Alberto Juantorena. I called him Alberto. Out we went and even though the Redditch opening attack was quite okay, in no time we were none-for-50, then none-for-70, then none-for-100. I never realised opening the batting was quite that easy. By the time the scoreboard reached none-for-130, I was about 70 and Alberto was 60-something, and at that point we were delayed by a brief shower. I'm not quite sure, but that might have been the first time in my career I'd ever had an innings of *mine* interrupted by rain.

We were only off for about 10 minutes, but during the break Harold, our skipper, came up and suggested it was time someone else had a dig. *That* had definitely never happened to me before. So when I went back I started swinging. I slogged at the first ball and it collided with the scoreboard. Six! Then another big blast over square-leg. Within two overs I was 95, just five away from my first ever century. I'd never even made a hundred in my dreams.

It was time to put up the shutters — I kicked a few away, scrambled a couple of singles, and then, with a judicious edge down to third man, I was there! It was awesome. Eventually, I finished 106 not out.

It was later in the same week that I received the amazing phone call from the then Australian team manager, the late Fred Bennett, telling me I was required to play in the Test at Old Trafford. Fred suggested during our conversation that when I arrived at the hotel I should come straight up to his room. It was in that room that I was introduced to the Australian captain, Kim Hughes, for the first time in my life. I remember when Kim shook my hand I called him 'Mr Hughes'.

One of the first things Kim asked me was where I should be batting. He would have known I wasn't all that capable, but I don't think he was all that familiar with my real ability. 'Well, I'm in pretty good form at the moment,' I told him. 'In fact, in my last innings I managed 106 not out.'

I didn't mention the fact it was a friendly match on a Wednesday against the Redditch cricket club.

'Is that right?' said Kim. 'Maybe you should bat in front of Clem.'

In the first innings I strolled out with the scoreboard showing 8–125, and trudged back at 9–126 after the local paceman Paul Allott (who was also making his Test debut) knocked my leg-stump out of the ground. It was my first Test duck. I must confess my display was not a good one, but I was surprised by the pace of the bowling. Paul Allott was a hell of a lot quicker than that bloke who'd opened the bowling for the team from Redditch!

Quite clearly my brief effort did little for the confidence of my captain and I was relegated down the order for the second innings. But I did much better the second time around, even though I didn't score a run — and thus became the first Australian to manage a pair on Test debut.

I batted with Allan Border for the best part of an hour in that second innings. We needed to bat for another 20 minutes and 20 overs more than that to save the game, but at least we gave it a decent shake. For much of the partnership we faced Botham and the 'offie', John Emburey, but eventually the English captain, Mike Brearley, brought back Bob Willis. I quickly learned that 'Bustling Bob' would have found little trouble winning a place in the Redditch XI. The first ball pitched short and outside off stump, but it seamed back, flew past my ribs, and Alan Knott behind the stumps caught it up around his chin. This was supposed to be a dead fifth-day wicket. He was a gun bowler was Bob Willis.

Not long after, a ball struck me high on the pad and fell towards Mike Gatting at short leg. He caught it, threw it high in the air and he and his team-mates walked off the field. And the ump gave me out! But I hadn't hit it, so I said I wasn't going — I was staying right where I was. But AB told me I had to go, and when I saw a few thousand Pommy cricket supporters charging towards the middle, I realised he was right.

I have a photo of the scene at Old Trafford after the match, taken from the pavilion balcony. An area had been roped off in front of the pavilion, which was where the post-match presentations were to take place. Around the roped-off area are the fans, many rows deep. You can see all the English players and AB standing in the presentation area, and a few of the Australians coming down as well. And amid the mass of English fans you can see me. Well, that's not exactly right. You *can't* actually see me. What you can see is a cricket bat held above the mob, looking for all the world like a submarine's periscope. I'm in the middle of the ruck, one hand firmly gripping the bat handle, trying to battle my way through.

•CHAPTER 17•

Always Keep Your
Eye on the Ball

The current Chairman of the Australian Cricket Board is Alan Crompton from NSW. A few seasons back, when Alan was a mere hard-working official with the NSW Cricket Association and a hard-working delegate to the ACB, he had the job of managing a NSW team on a journey to Hobart for a Shield match.

The match was played at the old Tasmanian Cricket Association Ground, one of the coldest and windiest places on Earth.

Alan had played first-grade cricket with Sydney University, but at this stage he was very much the non-playing solicitor. However, not long after we'd arrived at the ground the day before the game, he volunteered to help out in any way he could with fielding drills and the like.

'I've brought my tracksuit with me,' he told us. 'And I used to play a bit of baseball. Give me that baseball glove and I'll catch a few.'

With some trepidation, I handed him the mitt. For a while he was okay, though I gained the impression a few of the better fieldsmen might have been taking things a bit easy. Then one of our best arms let fly. Alan had time to get the mitt up about throat high, but the ball was *eyebrow* high and crashed through his pair of glasses into the lower part of his forehead.

Down he went. How he wasn't knocked out, maybe even killed, is beyond me. The frames of his glasses were shattered, and he had blood coming from a nasty cut smack between the eyebrows.

Now, I know this will sound bad, but because he was an official it was funny. While we were all laughing, one of the team walked up and, with Alan on the ground having the blood sponged from his face, took the mitt away from him.

'I think you might as well have a bit of a rest now, Mr Crompton,' he said. 'But we really appreciate all your help.'

The game started the next day, and a prominent figure missing from the pre-match warm-ups was A. Crompton. He was sitting quietly on the balcony outside the away-team dress-

ing room, dressed in a smart grey business suit, with a piece of clear sticky tape holding the two halves of his glasses together.

This was one of the more memorable matches I played in, largely because the Tassie paceman Peter Clough took one of the best-quality hat-tricks on record. The three victims were all Test players — John Dyson, Steve Smith and Trevor Chappell.

Later in the same game, one of our batsmen nicked their other 'quick', the champion West Indian Michael Holding, through to the keeper Roger Woolley. But the umpire gave it not out, which didn't impress Michael one bit. However, to his great credit, Michael Holding is not the type of bloke to cause a scene — even after such a blatant mistake. He didn't say a word, just looked at the batsman, the umpire, back at the batsman and then returned to his mark. When he finally made it there, he turned and began that majestic long run that was a trademark of the West Indian cricket team of that era. This delivery was about three metres quicker than the previous ball and was through to Woolley before the batsman had a chance to think. With that, the umpire called out confidently: 'Over.'

Michael walked over and took his hat and jumpers from the umpire. And as he did so he said quietly to the ump, in that very deep voice of his that viewers of Channel Nine's cricket coverage know so well:

'At least you can count to six.'

•CHAPTER 18•

Fielding on the Fence

I found myself in some bizarre situations while fielding at fine leg during my cricket career — there were occasions you would not believe. I had so many objects thrown at me by people in the crowd that the total would make up a very long list. Here goes . . . ice, coins, all sorts of rubbish, drinks (in plastic and glass bottles), cans (empty and full), apples, bananas, oranges, grapes, eskies, full chickens ('you guys aren't hungry today?'), ice creams, bread rolls (some still wrapped in Gladwrap), batteries, hot dogs, pies, abuse . . .

Yeah, abuse. I copped some lovely things over the years. When they bagged your bowling you could usually handle it. And when they sledged your family it was close to the bone . . . but you still *had* to wear it. If I had jumped the fence, Cantona-like, and belted the bloke who sledged me, I'd have been the one to pay the price. If you were out in the street and you were confronted with that sort of abuse, you'd be a mug not to belt the bloke. But then, the sort of bloke who abuses at the cricket wouldn't have the ticker to bag you on the street, to your face.

For some people at the cricket it's suddenly different to being in the real world. Commentators will drag out the cliche:

'They've paid their money, so they're entitled to shout.' Which implies they (the spectators) can shout anything.

I reckon that's complete bullshit.

The ones with the biggest and ugliest mouths are inevitably blokes who want to be where you are but haven't the talent or the dedication to get anywhere close. I used to look at them — they usually weighed about 200kg and were just polishing off the last of their daily quota of six pies and a dozen tinnies — and almost feel sorry. I could never relate to their mentality . . . the way they'd react during a one-day international, when I would be down at fine leg or third man, and if I knocked back the chance to give an autograph . . . *bang*, they were into me.

You have to understand that these fielding positions, especially third man, can be pretty busy going in a one-dayer. At third man, with only one slip (or maybe no slip at all), the batsmen are forever trying to glide the ball for one . . . or maybe two. From your point of view it has to be one. One might go a bit finer, or a bit squarer, and each time they turn the single into two your skipper is on your back, to make sure it doesn't happen again.

At times like this, I would turn to the autograph hunter behind the fence and quietly say: 'Mate, look, it's really hairy down here. They're working me hard. If I misfield one of these we could lose the game. Just give me an over or two, and if things lighten up a bit, I'll see what I can do.'

And what do they do? Abuse you, long and loud. Not all of them. But enough of them to make it unpleasant.

And when you do sign one, then inevitably there will be a queue formed in no time, usually young kids who were too reticent to ask in the first place but, having seen you give one autograph, now presume things are okay. I love giving kids my autograph; it's good for the ego, and I remember how I felt when I was a kid asking my favourite players for their signature. But you can't sign them all right away. The kids don't mind waiting, but not so the mindless bores around them. 'C'mon,

Whitney,' they would yell, inevitably with the old adjectives thrown in, 'who do you think you are?'

So then I would have to convince my captain I should be fielding somewhere else. Or stand there and cop the crap. Or if I did take my chances and tried to satisfy everyone, and then missed the ball when it came my way — and signing autographs is a foolproof way of making the ball come your way — imagine the garbage I would have copped from the angry patrons then . . . and later, from the selectors.

It's not just in the one-dayers that the insults can fly from beyond the boundary. I remember a day at the Adelaide Oval when I was playing for NSW in a Sheffield Shield game, when a collection of guys in a private box in the Sir Donald Bradman Stand, all of them wearing the latest in double-breasted suits, abused me long and loud all the way. They never let up, and some of it was more than a bit personal.

It was a typical Shield crowd — not too many — so their comments echoed across the ground. I guess they thought they were really clever. My first thought was: 'What a great adver-tisement for the insurance company who owned the box.' Does anyone really want such foul-mouthed people insuring their house, their car, their life?

By the end of the day, I'd had enough. After copping one last gobful as I walked off the ground, I decided to pay the box a visit. Instead of heading for the dressing room and a shower, I headed for the private box area. Through the members, round the back of the stands, up a flight of stairs, into the lift, found the right door, and knocked. And then the door opened. . .

The look on the faces inside made the trip worthwhile. The guy on the door went a very white shade of white. Conversation stopped. I might have been bowling all day, but all of a sudden they were sweating a lot more then I was.

'Have any of you blokes ever played cricket?' was the first thing I said.

One guy piped up: 'Yeah, I have.'

'Who for?'

'St Such-and-such in the such-and-such church comp.'

Which I guess made him a champion. 'Have you any idea what it's like to bowl all day, to slave all day, and all the time cop the kind of crap I've copped from you idiots?' I asked. 'I don't even know any of you people.'

No-one in the box said anything. It seemed they were a lot braver when I was on the other side of the fence. Then one of them asked me to stay for a beer. Okay, I said, but it was the quickest beer of my life. I thought those blokes were a disgrace — to the company that owned the box, to themselves . . . and to the game.

People in the midst of cricket crowds can behave in quite amazing ways. During another game in Adelaide, I was copping a caning from that very good South Australian opening bat, Glenn Bishop. While my bowling figures were heading from bad to worse, one particularly annoying voice from beyond the fence was succeeding in making my afternoon even grimmer. But the crazy thing was that, even though there was only a tiny crowd in and I could work out quite clearly where the stream of insults was coming from, I couldn't put a face to the voice. I'd be running into bowl, with a steady stream of obscene jibes keeping me company, but when I looked out after the ball was bowled to try and pinpoint where the shouts were coming from . . . there was no-one there.

So I asked my team-mate, John Dyson, to see if he could work it out. And what he told me had me shaking my head. Apparently there was a fellow in the outer, standing behind three people in front of the Victor Richardson Gates, who was yelling out, 'You're a c---, Whitney!' and then ducking down behind these other people so I wouldn't see him.

Not long after he was at it again. So, before I walked back to my bowling mark, I turned and pointed at him. And do you know what he did? Packed his bags, grabbed his blanket and went home. Straight to the exits, probably fearful I was right behind him. I wonder if he got his money's worth?

The worst crowd I ever played in front of was in Perth. I don't like bagging the place because it's a great city and I had some success there, but I must confess I used to absolutely hate going over there to play limited-overs matches for NSW. And there were a couple of times when playing for Australia that it wasn't all that friendly either. Some of the people at the WACA were occasionally parochial to the point of being painful. One day a bloke there even pulled a knife on me. Fair dinkum! It happened during a one-day match, not long after I'd taken seven wickets against the West Indies in Adelaide in early 1989. I was down at fine leg and this bloke, obviously pissed, was standing there, right on the fence, abusing me. Non-stop.

The WA crowd disliked NSW because we were the only team that ever beat them over there. And during the '80s we did it pretty often, in the Shield and in the one-dayers. While I was at fine leg, about three or four overs into this bloke's tirade, I turned around and said: 'Listen mate, all these people here have not paid their money to hear you abuse me.'

And you wouldn't believe it, everyone started yelling out: 'Yes we have!'

What do you do?

'Mate,' I said to this bloke, 'I'm just trying to play cricket and bowl . . .'

'You fuckin' bowl!' he slurred back. 'Fuck knows how you fluked those fuckin' wickets against the West Indies.'

So I told him to leave me alone and go and annoy someone else.

Not a chance. Instead he put his hand inside his jeans pocket and pulled out a pen-knife. By the time he finished folding the blade out I realised I was potentially in quite a bit of bother. 'I'm gonna fuckin' wait for you after the game,' he sneered at me. And then he explained what he was going to do with me.

I looked at the bloke and the look on his face and I was off.

I went up to Geoff Lawson and said: 'Henry, you've got to get me out of there. Some lunatic just pulled a knife out of his kick and said he's going to cut my guts out.'

'Sounds delightful, Roy,' said Henry.

Weird sense of humour has our captain. 'Why don't you go down to fine leg at the other end.'

So I was happy enough about that . . . for the best part of five minutes. But you wouldn't believe it, within a couple of overs he was down behind my back again. 'You think you can get away from me but you can't,' was all he said. Fortunately, eventually, he went away. But it was still a very quick and cautious dash for M. Whitney from the WACA dressing room to the team bus after the game.

However, I'm happy to report that fielding on the boundary is not all about bad times. Sydney was usually outstanding, except in the early days in front of the old Hill, when the old autograph problem came up occasionally. But in front of the Bradman stand and the Members' and the Brewongle stands — the people there were great and very loyal. And once the Hill fans got to know me, they were very good to me. More than once, the Sydney fans were able to pick me up . . . give me a lift.

I remember, however, making one big error in Sydney. One day someone threw a banana onto the field. It looked all right, too, so I picked it up, peeled it back and munched away.

Big, big mistake. The crowd went 'YEESSS!!!' and suddenly fruit was raining down from everywhere. Plums, peaches, apples. It was as if I was on the biggest Vitamin C kick of all time. 'It's okay folks, I only wanted one bite of the banana,' I gestured, but it was too late. Play had to be delayed while they cleaned the place up. If I'd set up a stand at that moment I could have run the biggest fruit market in Sydney.

The best fine leg I ever fielded was at Sabina Park in Kingston, Jamaica. It was magic, even if they were always saying: 'Curtly gonna kill you today, man.'

That was usually followed by: 'But dat cool, Whitney . . . 'cause you can't bat anyway!'

Then they all laughed. And I laughed with them.

I remember holding hands through the wire fence with a little girl called Kameal. All day, whenever I was down there. And I remember the Bob Marley music which sang out amid the rum and the dope. It was just great fun.

But the thing that really blew me out was their knowledge of the game.

'Thamsaan, Jeff Thamsaan,' they would shout out, 'what Thamsaan doin' now?'

I'd explain that he had just been appointed as coach of the Queensland Shield team. They had memories of Thommo's bowling in the late '70s, when he toured twice, first with Bobby Simpson's 'official' team and then with World Series Cricket.

'Whooooo! He WAS quick!! Whooooo!' they would drool.

And then they'd break into a 'Lilleeee . . . Lilleeee . . .' chant.

Although Jamaica was tops, fielding on the fence was a marvellous experience in every game I played on that tour. The thing I really appreciated about the West Indian crowds was that there was no animosity in the way they followed the game. But they used to go berserk when a bouncer was bowled. 'YEESSS!!' they would roar. They loved to see the short pill. From the first game in St Kitts to the last game in Antigua.

If there weren't enough being bowled they'd demand some more. 'Short bawl! Pitch de short bawl!' they'd yell. And if someone got hit it was pandemonium. They love their cricket, they know all the players and they go to the ground to have a real day out.

One thing I'll never forget were the light appeals of the fans in Jamaica. It was getting late on the second day and the home team was batting. As the sun made its way towards the horizon, and the light dimmed, the local spectators decided it was too dark. To make their point, they began lighting rolled up newspapers, as if they were about to enter a dark cave in a horror movie. Within minutes, it seemed as if every single person beyond the fence had his or her own torch. And, with the side-effects now in place, they began yelling out to the umpires: 'Too dark . . . too dark, umpire . . . too dark.'

Now Sabina Park in Kingston, Jamaica, is not the most modern stadium in the world of cricket. Most of the seating is made of timber, the stands are made of timber, and this strategy of the fans seemed at least a little risky. Just a little puff of wind, a bit of red-hot ash, and the whole ground might have been up in flames. But no-one seemed to care. In the spectators' opinion it was too dark and this was the way to catch the umpires' attention.

'Too dark . . . too dark . . . time to go!'

Not long afterward, we were off.

•CHAPTER 19•

Talk Me Through That One

Batsmen have a misconception that they are the ones who are constantly hard done by in this game of cricket. That's garbage. For example, the records say Mike Whitney took 412 wickets in his first-class career; I reckon if the umps had had *any* idea at all I'd have finished with closer to 600. I once asked Geoff Lawson about this and he said he actually took around 2000 wickets.

Umpires are always making mistakes with the lbws!

What about this for instance? One day I was bowling in a league match in England when I heard what remained throughout my career to be the most bizarre reason for a not out ever given by an umpire.

I was coming over the wicket and bowling these big inswingers. A new batsman came in, and I thought, first ball, I'll get him with a yorker. When I let the thing go, it was quickly apparent the bloke with the bat in his hand had different ideas. He just pushed his back foot across the crease and shaped to hook. Someone must have told him I was going to start with a bouncer.

The ball started about six inches outside the line of off-stump, and then swung back. The poor batsman had no chance.

With his weight on his back foot, and his bat coming across the line, he didn't have a hope of re-adjusting and the ball struck him on the big toe, right above the point where just a few seconds earlier he'd marked his middle-stump guard on the popping crease.

I didn't so much as appeal as charge down the wicket, right arm high in the air. I was well on the way to a decent wicket haul, and a healthy collection from my hometown fans. But then I realised something was wrong and I slowly turned to see the umpire standing quietly behind the bowler's end stumps, hands in his dustcoat pockets, grey cap hiding his eyebrows, totally unmoved.

It was soon apparent he had just declined to give out the most obvious lbw in the history of the game. 'Excuse me, ump,' I said. 'How about talking me through that one.'

He looked up at me from beneath his cap. 'Ah lad,' he replied slowly. 'You're onlooky. But I was playin' in game when I was umpirin' 20 years ago, when lad bowled yorker. Yorker hit divot where batsman mark guard, and leapt over stumps. So I can't be sure that when you 'it 'im up there just now in same spot that it goin' 'it stumps.'

I just stared at him. 'Are you serious, mate?'

'Ah, lad, I'm fookin' serious. Ball 'it divot, leapt over, and you're up there just now . . .'

'That was 20 years ago!'

'Ah lad, but still mark up there where they're hittin' ground.'

In first-class matches in Australia, there are basically two types of umpires. There are the ones who, after you've asked them to 'talk me through that one', will say: 'pitched two inches outside the stumps.' Or maybe an inch.

And you think: 'An inch?'

That's not bad eyesight. After all, the ball's travelling at around 85 miles an hour. No wonder blokes like that are umpires.

But at least they'll talk to you. Then there are the umpires who'll say, after you ask: 'Talk me through that one?'

'Not out.'

'Pardon?'

'NOT OUT!!'

That used to really annoy me. I think those sort of umpires just want to assert their authority. I've had umpires no-ball me in the first over of a game, yet when I've looked at the popping crease there's not a sprig mark over the line. There might have been three balls bowled, and I can clearly see all three boot marks and they're all clearly behind the line. But I've been no-balled. And when you ask how this has happened, the ump just stands with his arm outstretched, oblivious to your query. They might just repeat, in an outrageously inappropriate school-master's voice: 'No ball.' I could only guess that they want everyone to know they're in the game.

I know it's a tough job and I know every decision is high-lighted by the media, but I could never see anything wrong with umpires being human. However, many of the umps I encountered over the years were great. Steve Randell from Tasmania is a good bloke. Always had a jelly bean in his pocket, and he'd call me Whit. 'Hey, Whit,' he'd say, 'one ball to go.'

Tony Crafter was the same. I'd always have a good time with 'TC'. I can remember a Shield match in Adelaide where Darren Lehmann belted the Blues attack for a magnificent double century. Gee, it was a great dig, but it shouldn't have been 200, because I had him caught behind, off the glove, when he was about 180. I'd been bowling for ever, so when I finally got him, I was pretty happy, and more than a bit relieved. But Tony Crafter gave him not out.

'What was the problem with that, TC?' I asked through clenched teeth.

'Sorry, Whit,' Tony replied. 'I gave it the way I saw it.'

After the day's play, Tony sought me out. I told him I was really disappointed but he just said again: 'Whit, I'm only reading it from where I am and I didn't think he hit it.'

'Mate,' I said, 'if that's your conviction, you were 100 per cent right.'

'And,' I added, 'I appreciate you having a word to me about it.'

I think that most people, including maybe an international referee or two, have little, if any, perception of what *really* happens on the cricket field. Take the example of Shane Warne at the Wanderers Ground in Johannesburg during the first Test of Australia's tour to South Africa in early 1994. As we all know, the television cameras displayed an ugly scene — of Shane running towards and then abusing the local opening bat, Andrew Hudson. It was an incident that led to Shane paying a hefty fine and was often used by those critics who wanted to paint the Australians as a rude, poorly-behaved team.

Sure, the incident was bad. It was bad for the young cricket fans watching — the kids who have Shane Warne posters hung above their beds. They're the first ones I think of when I see that sort of thing. However, there's another side to this story. I played more than 10 years of first-class cricket, and I witnessed, on many an occasion, the guy at the non-striker's end giving the bowler an absolute mouthful between deliveries and between overs. Read what follows, and as you do, add as many different expletives as you can think of where I've left the gaps. 'You ------- -----,' they'd start, 'you think you're ------- number one. Well I'm going to knock you all round the ------- ground.' That sort of thing is not pretty, but it does happen, and it's never picked up by the lurking television cameras.

I can remember one leading Australian batsman of the early '80s who was an absolute classic at this. He'd stand at the bowler's end, sitting on his bat, while some young guy tried to establish himself in the Sheffield Shield. 'Ho! Ho! Ho!' this bloke would chortle. 'Happy -------- birthday!' To his chuckling partner at the other end he'd call out: 'Can you believe this crap?' He wouldn't even back up, just sit on his bat. 'There's no need for it,' he'd tell everyone. 'It's Christmas time. We're only hitting fours!'

I've had batsmen say to me: 'I hope you're still sending down that ------ tripe when I'm down the other end.' Now if I had knocked that bloke over in the following minutes, should I have run over to him and said 'bad luck, matey,' and then sent him on his way with a friendly tap on the shoulder?

Not quite!

I'm not saying this is the sort of thing that was happening when Warney had his trouble in Johannesburg. But it might have been. It's something cricket fans should consider next time they're bagging an Aussie cricketer for his behaviour on the field. Just remember, our opponents aren't angels either.

Take the boys from Pakistan. I can recall two of them conversing with each other during a game — one was fielding at second slip, the other at extra cover — in their native

107

language of Urdu. I couldn't understand a word, except for the last one . . .'WHITNEY!' . . . which was spat out in the same tone a bank robber might use the teller's name after he's asked for the cash. There's no way the part that didn't make any sense was complimentary.

I turned to the bloke in the covers and said: 'What's your problem? If you're going to bag me, bag me, but do it in English, you bastard.'

Then they all started running around, arms and tongues going everywhere, screaming: 'Don't you call us bastard, you bastard Whitney!' At the disciplinary hearing afterwards, the Pakistani that was cited threw his hands up and claimed it couldn't have been him because he didn't speak English. And anyway, he shouldn't have to take the abuse he'd copped from that bastard Whitney, which apparently he couldn't understand.

And then I'd pay my fine.

•CHAPTER 20•

'Because I'm the Umpire, That's Why!'

One very cold and windy day in the north of England in 1983, I was bowling in a league match for Littleborough. The wind was so strong that the bails were forever being blown off the stumps. Now in most matches that take place in a gale, the umpires eventually decide to take the bails out of the game. But not this time.

Instead one of the umpires pulled from out of his pocket two lengths of very thick string, about 30 centimetres long. Tied to the ends of each piece of string were big steel nuts, and in a very precise manner this ump placed the string over each bail at his end.

He was your typical north-of-England league ump. A stumpy old bloke, with an off-white coat, grey cap, gruff manner and few words. If he didn't work down a coal mine himself, he knew plenty of people who did. And even though he was an umpire, he looked as tough as nails. 'Hey mate,' I said to him as he put the string over the bails, 'you can't do that!'

'Yes I can,' he mumbled back.

'How can you . . .' I began to complain.

'I can do what I fookin' like. I'm th'umpire.'

Not long after, I bowled a bloke, all ends up. And one of

the bails just took off. The string and nuts wrapped around it, and . . . wooOOOSH!!! . . . it flew towards our slip cordon like a rock out of a slingshot. Looking back, it was fortunate no-one was killed. The general consensus among the players was that the string and nuts were not a good idea, but quite clearly the ump did not agree. While the dismissed batsman headed for the warmth of the pavilion, the little ump slowly walked down to third man to collect the bail, string and nuts, then walked back and placed them back where they belonged.

The bails didn't blow off for the rest of the afternoon.

Seven years later, during my third season in the north of England (this time for Haslingden), I was required to play a game at a remote and extremely cold place called Bacup. Among their throng of local supporters, Bacup had a bloke who went by the name of 'Roy of Rosindale', and quickly proved he was at least one sandwich short of a picnic. No sooner had I bowled my first delivery when this bloke is yelling out: 'Hey he looks like Whitneee Hooosten!! Hey Whitneee Hooosten!!'

'Who the bloody hell is *that*?' I asked a colleague.

'That's Roy of Rosindale,' I was told. 'He's been drivin' us mad for years.'

Then I dropped a tough caught and bowled and I was no longer 'Whitneee Hooosten'.

I was . . .'Whitneee Useless!!'

Charming. And he never let up . . . all day. Rosindale, I was told, was the name of the valley in which the town of Bacup was located. Unfortunately we lost the game, and afterwards in the home team's clubhouse we copped a gobful from the home fans, and especially from Roy of Rosindale. 'Whitneee Useless!!' he kept crying out. 'Whitneee bluddy Useless!!'

My team-mates kept telling me to ignore him, but after a while I'd had enough.

'Hey, Roy,' I yelled back at him, 'what do you do for a living?'

'Well, Mr Whitneee bluddy Useless,' he chortled back, 'I make shoes.'

'So I don't tell you how to make shoes. How about leaving out the advice about how to bowl left arm?'

He stopped to think about that for a second, started to say something, stopped again and then said . . .

'I s'pose you're right.'

And then he went back to his pint, and I never heard another word out of him all night. But three weeks later we had to return for a Cup match and Roy was back behind the fence, from the very first ball . . .

'Hey, it's Whitneee bluddy Useless!!!'

Roy of Rosindale wasn't the only gentleman from the Northern Leagues who wasn't swimming between the flags. I remember one game in which I copped a mouthful from a group of opposition supporters from the first ball of the match to the last. After the last wicket fell and we'd won the game, I charged across, looked straight at them, and roared: 'Okay, which one of you blokes called me a bastard?' In no time they all had their right hands up in the air, which wasn't quite what I'd had in mind. If I was going to have a blue I only wanted to take on one or two of them.

'All right then,' I said calmly, 'I want to see all you bastards in the bar in a minute so I can buy you all a beer.'

We ended up getting very drunk that night.

Some of the loudest critics claimed they were on your side. There's a group of supporters at Haslingden who go by the name of 'The Panel'. My first league game for them in 1990 was at East Lancashire, where Paul Reiffel was the local pro, and the game reached the stage where they needed about seven or eight an over to win. We shouldn't have had too much trouble sealing the win, but I was still a bit rusty and a veteran South African bloke started carting me around the place. For about five or six overs it looked like the home side might even pull off a remarkable come-from-behind victory.

Every time I ran down to fine leg after bowling an over during this exciting climax there was a group of old timers who persisted in giving me a gobful. 'Bowlin' crap you are,' they would sneer, 'fookin' pitch it up.' And then they'd murmur to each other, with a shake of the head . . .

'Fookin' dud buy.'

After a few minutes of this constant criticism, I had to say something. 'Look fellas,' I said, 'gimme a break. If you want to bag your East Lancs blokes, that's fine. But leave me out of it.'

'Hey what?' one of them said indignantly. 'We're not from East bluddy Lancs. We're supportin' 'Aslingden!'

These old blokes were 'The Panel' — a collection of about four or five (there used to be more) veteran followers of Haslingden's cricket team, who for many, many years had been travelling to games to applaud when the team was playing well and barrack when the team was going badly. This in itself sounds fine, but The Panel always seemed to enjoy bagging their players a lot more than cheering them. And they were brilliant at delivering that very dreadful line: 'You're not as good as they were in our day.'

During one season in the '80s, Haslingden's pro was the Zimbabwean, Eddo Brandes. Unfortunately Eddo, who'd been signed primarily as a bowler, had a very ordinary summer with the ball, but he made up for it by scoring a lot of runs. And he scored them very quickly. But The Panel had been told he was a bowler, so they barracked him unmercifully . . . game after game after game. By the time of about the third last match of the season, Eddo had copped enough, and after suffering a very rare failure with the bat (after which The Panel booed him from the field) he walked up to them, still wearing his pads and gloves, and but for the restraining arms of a few of his team-mates, would have done more damage to The Panel's numbers than the two Wars and old age had managed in the previous 70 years.

Littleborough, the team I played for in 1983, also had a tiny but very vocal group of veteran home-town fans. In fact, by the time I arrived in town there were only three of them still alive, and they went by the name of 'The Muppets'. To them, everything that happened out on the field was either wrong or wrong. That field placing was wrong. That shot he played was wrong. The bowling was wrong for that type of wicket. So was the batting. Even the ball that smashed all three stumps out of the bloody ground was wrong.

But don't get me wrong. Unlike The Panel, who I considered to be a group of cranky old men, The Muppets were good blokes who liked to have a beer with you, share in the victories and suffer in the defeats. But they always had an opinion which always seemed to be contrary to what was happening out on the field.

Some of the situations I found myself in in league cricket were bizarre. While at Littleborough, we played at Oldham, not far from Manchester, and the fog was so thick you couldn't see the middle from the pavilion. It was only after a wind came up and blew the fog away that I realised there actually was a game of cricket going on. At a place called Hyde we played in Arctic conditions, and were hailed off the ground twice — hardly cricket weather — but that wasn't the only crazy thing about the place. The ground was situated right on top of a mountain, and they reckoned that on a clear day you could see five different counties. Mind you, as I was told about this while we sat round a log fire as some pretty serious hail crashed down on the pavilion roof, this didn't seem all that relevant. At one end, they didn't need a sightscreen — except on the very dark days the sky did the job (and on the very dark days the bowlers were going to get you out whether there was a sightscreen there or not).

At Norden's home ground, the backyard of a property that adjoins the ground protrudes so far onto the playing field that the fielding positions of gully and deep third man are one and the same thing. It's the only ground in the world where a slip

113

catch has been disallowed because the slipper fell over the boundary while taking the catch.

I remember one guy from my days at Littleborough who I'd struck under the chin early in an innings and who came back later wearing a helmet but with the strap undone. I thought at the time he didn't have the strap done up because he hated the thought of having to wear a lid, but maybe it had something to do with the fact that his jaw was broken in five places.

I looked at him as he was standing at the non-striker's end, and said: 'You're kidding, mate. You know if you're stupid enough to come out here I'm going to bounce you.'

The poor guy was not a pretty sight, but fortunately he immediately had a swing at our spinner and was caught, after which he headed straight for the local hospital, where he spent the next five weeks, with his jaw tightly wired.

Ten years later I received a letter from my captain that season at Littleborough, a bloke called Ray Hill. He went on for a while about most of the usual things — how are you, hear you and Debbie had triplets, hope everyone is well and so on — before he mentioned he'd bumped into that same unlucky batsman. 'Remember that fellow whose jaw you broke back in '83,' Ray wrote. 'I ran into him in Manchester just the other day, and guess what . . . he's still ugly!!'

•CHAPTER 21•

The Randwick Wanderers

My first journey out of Australia was with a combination of cricketers called the Randwick Wanderers, who in 1978 set out on a six-week tour of Great Britain. This was the event that really launched my cricket career, because it wasn't until that trip that I realised that such a thing as a fair dinkum cricket career was a real possibility. In many ways it was this trip, rather than my selection in the Australian team in 1981, that was the important event of my entire cricketing life.

In 1978, I was in my second year as an apprentice ground engineer with Qantas and an extremely raw fourth-grade fast bowler with the Randwick Cricket Club. The club had organised a tour of the UK for their members and friends and I wanted to be a part of it. I had the money I needed, but as I had only been with Qantas for 12 months, I didn't have enough leave due for the entire trip. So in I went to see the personnel manager, a bloke by the name of Mr Parsons, to try and bludge an extra two weeks' annual leave.

'You really like this cricket business, don't you Michael?' said Mr Parsons, who looked a picture in his brown suit, green body shirt and yellow-and-brown striped tie.

'Yes sir,' I replied. 'I'm going really well, playing fourth grade for Randwick, opening the bowling, hoping to make thirds next year with a bit of luck. This off-season trip to England could really help my chances.'

I was sure the trip would boost my cricket. But the main reason I was going was because I'd hurt my knee in a pre-season football trial. The knee was too shaky for football, but certainly wasn't bad enough to keep me out of a cricket trip and a chance to see a little bit of the world.

'You realise you're asking for two weeks out of your second year's leave?' asked Mr Parsons.

'I know that, sir, but the opportunity is a . . .'

'Okay,' said Mr Parsons.

I couldn't believe it. I could not believe he had said: 'Okay.'

'Thank you. Thanks, Mr Parsons. I'll be a good boy. I promise I'll work hard at tech . . .'

I had the forms filled out in a flash — before he could change his mind.

There were 22 of us in all, and we all put our heads down and practised hard at former England Test player Barry Knight's indoor centre in the city. We also devoted a fair amount of our spare minutes to organising raffles and gambling nights to minimise the cost of the trip. My expenses were limited even further because I was a Qantas employee. One of the perks of working for the company was the availability of extremely cheap (as in 90 per cent off) flights, so long as you had worked for a minimum of 12 months with them which I had, just. From my point of view, of course, this was a perfect arrangement, and I set off to London a couple of days before the rest of the touring party.

I had to allow that couple of days grace because there was always a chance that, if the flight became full, I would have to change flights at one of the stopovers, and wait as a standby passenger. This could have added days to my journey. But I was lucky, and flew straight to Heathrow.

Well, it was almost straight to Heathrow. In truth, I had to fly Sydney to Singapore, then change planes and head for Bombay, and then wait for a third plane to get me to London. But none of the gaps were of any great length, so the actual time spent flying between Sydney and London was not much more than normal.

While I was waiting at my first touchdown point, I hooked up with some other airline staff who were playing the same game as me, and we travelled as a gang of five from Singapore to Bombay. There, we had to disembark and wait for confirmation there were vacant seats for us to get to London. For a while it looked very dodgy, which for one of the girls in the group would have been a disaster because she really needed to get to London as quickly as she could. It was only at the very last second we were told there would be room, and we were quickly escorted by an Air India official through a passageway

and out onto the edge of the tarmac. There we were told to wait, while the little fella from Air India sorted things out with the security guards. Not too far away, we could see our plane sitting in the Bombay sunshine.

Unfortunately, our friend who needed to get to London in a hurry didn't hear the request to stop, and she charged out onto the tarmac. But she didn't get far, as one of the security guys turned around and stiff-armed her with his rifle butt. Straight across the chest! And down she went, like a shot duck in a shooting gallery.

So this is what the rest of the world is like, thought Michael Roy Whitney!

Fortunately, the girl was more stunned than anything else and after a few tears and a mouthful of advice to the guy who'd thumped her, we all proceeded to board the plane and head off to London.

When I arrived, I grabbed my bags, took a deep breath, and set out into the great unknown. I had two days in one of the great historic cities of the world . . . on my own.

Now this might seem fairly ho-hum for you seasoned travellers out there, but to a young bloke alone in a strange city two or three universes from home, it was all very intimidating.

The first thing I did was hail a cab to get me from Heathrow to the hotel where the team would be staying in London. If you've been to London, you'll know that's a bloody expensive fare. But no-one had told me about the train link, and anyway, as far as I was concerned Heathrow to the centre of London was just like Mascot to the centre of Sydney. About 15 minutes maximum. By the time the cabbie woke me up to tell me we'd arrived at the hotel, I was about three days behind in my budget.

Then came a further jolt at the hotel reception. When you hand over your cheque to pay for an overseas tour of this kind, you don't get a breakdown of what each night's accommodation is worth. So I had no idea what the hotel was going to charge for the extra nights. My experience with the cost of a night's accommodation went no further than the cost of a room in old pubs when we'd gone on surfing tours up or down the coast of NSW — about five bucks, a few 20-cent pieces through the pinnies and a hamburger with cheese and bacon for dinner. Now here was this stuffed-up pommy in a fancy outfit telling me he wanted another three days of my budget so I could stay at his hotel. But I had no choice. This was the only hotel I knew in London, and even if there were any more, I assumed they all charged the same exorbitant rates.

Once I got over the shock and disappointment of my empty wallet, I set out on a stroll through the streets of London. I walked past Marble Arch, then up Oxford Street and the thing that immediately hit me was the number of people on the street. How huge was this joint? It seemed as if every minute there was like Sydney on Christmas Eve.

I took in landmarks such as Speakers' Corner, Harrods, Big Ben, Trafalgar Square, St Paul's Cathedral and had my debut ride on the London tube. After a few hours, I ran into a group of locals who seemed keen to introduce themselves. They were, one of them said, from a place called the Church of Scientology. I had never heard of them and assumed they were some local religious group who somehow hadn't made it out to Australia. I didn't really care about their beliefs at all but their promise of a free meal and drinks was very tempting, especially given my problems with cabs and hotel bills. So I tagged along back to their headquarters, where I tucked into a feed that was just about worth what I paid for it. Then they tried to hit me with their spiel, but all I said was: 'What about that drink you promised me?' When they replied, 'Oh yeah, what type of juice would you like?' I knew the Church of Scientology wasn't for me. Not long afterwards, despite their pleas and veiled threats, I was back on the street.

The following day I met, for the first time in my life, some people from Scotland. Looking back now, I realise that these two blokes were not your typical Scots, but at the time I assumed they were, and this meant that Scotland was a bloody crazy country. I ran into them in Hyde Park, where I'd gone for a stroll, just near the Serpentine lake that dominates the centre of the park.

In the thickest Scottish accent I will ever hear in my life, one of them asked: 'Whered'fookin'ell'reyoufrumthen?'

'Australia,' I replied, which I must admit was something of a guess answer, as I really had no idea what he'd said.

'Fookin' Aussie, eh!' I think they both screamed.

It transpired that these two gentlemen were planning a quick trip around the lake on one of the boats that were available for hire. Would I like to join them? No problem.

At first, I was given the job with the oars but then one of the Scots took over . . . and started ramming the other boats. Fair dinkum! I remember one young couple having their romantic little Sunday away from the pressures of the real world rudely interrupted by our boat crunching into them. It was probably the first time the lady had ever heard her gentlemanly boyfriend swear. And, boy, he gave us a mouthful. My new friends just laughed and laughed. This went on for a while, but soon they were bored and they headed for shore, which is where they performed their final act.

They sank the boat. About five metres from the bank they began rocking the boat until it had so much water in it that it slowly sank beneath the waves. And then, with a swagger, they walked away. And I followed. This really was a weird country I'd landed in.

On this, my first night in Great Britain, I had my first experience of an English pub, enjoying a few pints of lager and a meal at a place called the 'Black Swan'. By the time the boys arrived from Australia I was a seasoned veteran and quickly recommended the place. It might have been the only pub I'd ever been to outside of NSW, but I knew it was very British and that the locals were a good bunch of blokes. It was only later that I learned that there are a thousand and one pubs in the United Kingdom exactly the same as the Black Swan.

London made a huge impression on me. Things I had only ever read about actually existed and were even more awesome than I had imagined. Once my team-mates were settled into the hotel the adventure continued and I inspected Buckingham Palace, the Tower of London, Westminster Abbey. And then we began playing cricket . . . and having a fabulous time.

Unfortunately, my tour started with a bit of a hiccup. Our first journey, by bus, was from our London hotel to Windsor, the site of one of the Queen's many plush residences, Windsor Castle. It was only a short day trip, and we were leaving at 7 o'clock in the morning as the plan was to have the official team photo taken with the magnificent castle in the background, before we set off for a local cricket ground for our first match.

The only trouble was, I didn't spend the night before the Windsor trip at the team hotel. Sadly, I was sidetracked at the Black Swan, and ended up at a flat somewhere in London. When I woke the next day, I grabbed for my watch which read . . . 7.30. This was not good.

First I had to work out where I was, then I had to catch a train back to our hotel. By the time I got there it was 8.15am. 'They didn't leave until 7.45,' explained the guy at reception. 'They were waiting for someone.'

I raced up to my room, grabbed my gear, and after a quick tip from a local, headed for Victoria Station, to catch a train for Windsor.

Not until I arrived in Windsor did I realise that there was absolutely no way I was going to find the team. For the last few kilometres into Windsor station all I seemed to see were fields with bloody cricket pitches in the middle of them. I hadn't a clue where they were playing. And Windsor was not a tiny village, it was a fairly substantial town. For a while, about 30 minutes, I walked forlornly around the city centre with my cricket kit slung over my shoulder. Then I gave up and headed for a pub, where I sat at the window and cried into a pint. I'd let my mates down. There was no way I was ever going to find my team.

I would have only been there five minutes when the impossible happened. The lads marched past my window. I banged on the glass as hard as I could, and then watched with a grin as they walked in. By the looks on their faces, they quite clearly couldn't believe I was there.

'Where the hell have you been?' I asked with just a hint of exasperation (I didn't want to push my luck too far). 'I've been waiting ages for you blokes!'

After an eventful day in Windsor, we returned to London (I decided to come back on the bus rather than catch the train back). From there we headed to Bournemouth on the south coast to start an odyssey that took in the midlands, Wales, Lancashire, Scotland, Durham, Yorkshire, the east coast and finally London again. Early on, we played a game on the manor of the Duke of Cornwall. The field we played on was a small slice of a huge property that featured a magnificent mansion, servants' quarters, immaculate stables, and even the Duke's own private stream complete with his own trout. This was a world far removed from what I had ever known, yet the cricketers we played against and shared an ale with after the game were no better or worse than ourselves in ability, and enjoyed the game just as much.

I was stunned by the beauty of some of the towns and districts we passed through. The Lakes District in the north of England, for example, is a very special place. There were two towns in that area, Ambleside and Grassmere, that I'll never forget, the houses there built of shale and stone, in a style that has you thinking you're walking through a huge dolls' village. The main streets are dotted with little shops, with flowers outside, that specialise in local crafts and pottery. These places were as distant from the hustle of London as was the world in

Sydney's eastern suburbs where I had grown up. It was all so different to what I was accustomed to.

The cricket we played throughout the tour was always enjoyable; sometimes we met sides slightly above our standard, at other times we had to go easy to avoid embarrassing our hosts. I recall one bloke walking out to face me without so much as a pad on. When I pointed out that if I hit him on the leg it might sting a bit he just said: 'Ah, don't worry, just fookin' bowl.' I didn't go easy on him — and it did sting a bit. Inevitably every post-match celebration featured what amounted to a 'skull-a-thon', as the locals challenged the Aussie invaders to test their drinking skills. We struggled early on to come to grips with the extra demands of the pint glass but once acclimatised to the local bitter, which is less gassy than the European lagers we'd started off on, we showed our style and produced some magnificent performances.

At times we did some awful things, but then we were young men abroad in search of a very good time. More than one tourist lost his pants in the name of fun and I can even remember one guy's gear ending up in a piano in a nice bar located in the ritziest part of London. By the time this incident occurred we were staying in a flash hotel in St James, preparing for our flight home. The guy in question was a quiet lad, who'd tended to avoid most of the wild things that had gone on during the trip, so we decided to give him a farewell to remember us by. We lurked in the hotel corridor while one of the guys tried to lure him out of his room. After the knock on his door, his face appeared for no more than a second but that was enough and we jumped him, and dragged him kicking and screaming to the lifts.

On the way down all his gear was ripped off, so that by the time we reached ground he was as naked as the day he was born. We punted him out, hit the 'close door' button, and left him with the opportunity to introduce himself to the elegant ladies and distinguished gentlemen who had congregated in the hotel foyer.

Meanwhile, the first floor bar was chosen as the perfect place to celebrate the success of our prank, but once we got there one bloke asked: 'What do you want me to do with these?' 'These' being his clothes. We looked around for a minute and then someone pointed to this magnificent grand piano in the corner beside the dance floor. It was perfect and our team-mate's favourite outfit was quickly tucked away within the glistening timber body of the piano. We ordered a round of drinks and waited, and about half an hour later our now re-clothed friend arrived, demanding to know what we'd done with his gear. But we didn't let on until the following morning, although we did find time to return to the bar later that night, to see if the shirt, trousers, jocks and socks made any difference to the sound of the music tinkling from the keyboard.

In Worcestershire we stayed in this place called Droitwich, where we spent a night on the turps before returning to our hotel early the following morning. There were 10 of us, all less than sober, and we clambered into the lift for a journey to the third floor, where the team was housed. I can clearly remember still having a full pint in my hand. Unfortunately, about three-quarters of the way up, the old conveyance spluttered to a halt and we were left hanging in mid-stream. The bloke closest to the 'open door' button started giving it a belting, until he noticed a notice on the lift wall which read: 'Maximum Loading — 6 adults'. By the time he'd read it out the second time we were as stationary as 10 drunk cricketers in a tiny lift can be. The middle of the English countryside at three in the morning didn't seem exactly the right place and time to die.

Not only were there 10 blokes in the lift, but one or two of them were pretty *big* blokes. And as we quickly learned, one of them was claustrophobic. 'Hey! Hey!' he began yelling out. 'Where's the manager? Where's the manager?' And then one of those things that generally happen when you've had too much to drink happened to me — I needed to go to the gents. And have you ever noticed in these situations how, the more you try not to think about it, the more pressing the need becomes?

Standing down in the lift foyer was another of our party, who we'd left at the pub we'd been drinking at so he could get knocked back by a local lass. This had duly happened. He could hear the racket coming from the broken lift (we had the doors of the lift opened by this stage) and, after about five minutes of drunken deliberation, went and woke the hotel manager. When the boss arrived, clearly less than impressed, he managed to force the ground floor doors open just enough to stick his head through so he could have a look up. But, unfortunately, it was just at this moment that I realised there was no possible way I was going to hang on until we escaped. The obvious happened. The hotel manager started peering up at us just as I began peeing down and he copped the lot. To make matters worse, once I realised what I'd done, I threw the contents of the pint glass out of the lift as well, as if that was going to somehow cleanse things. The poor bloke was aled on as well as pissed on.

Eventually, we were rescued — and no sooner were we out of the lift than we were out of the hotel as well. For some strange reason the manager decided he didn't want us staying at his place any longer.

The tour was a fabulous experience, not only in terms of my cricket but for my life as well. I learned a lot about looking after myself, about growing up and about the things that men do. Most of the guys were a lot older than me — in their mid-20s and more — and even though they often told us that we young blokes were leading them astray, in truth it was more the reverse.

The tour also gave me an opportunity to play a couple of games with the Surrey Second XI, through a connection between that county and the Randwick club. Surrey needed a player for a match between the Second XI and the county staff. A bloke at Surrey had played a season at Randwick and knew we were in England, I was asked to play and took 4–40, and then was invited to play for the Second XI in a three-day match against

Combined Universities. When I did okay in that game as well, my name was mentioned in the press back in Australia — as a lad with some potential. Put simply, my cricket career was on its way. When I read those clippings in the weeks after I made it back home, and thought about the way cricket had given me a chance to see just a tiny bit of the world, I started to think seriously about cricket being more than just a series of Sydney Saturday afternoons in summer.

I decided I wanted to succeed in cricket, that I wanted to see more of the world. One final adventure on that tour fired my second ambition even further. On the way home after the tour, I spent 12 hours in Frankfurt with another squad member, Allan 'Corky' Cripps, whose brother worked for the German airline, Lufthansa, and was also able to secure cheap flights. Corky is a Randwick C.C. legend, the scorer of more runs for the club than anyone. In 1978 he was about 50, I was 19, and to spend a day sightseeing around a foreign city with him was an education in itself.

Now Frankfurt's not a bad joint, but it ranks nowhere near some of the really great old German cities that I have visited in the years since that first overseas adventure. But to me at that time it was almost mind-boggling. This was the first time I'd been in a city where everyone spoke a language different to the only one I knew. Signs I needed to read were in German, so I had to guess what they meant. It became a game working out the conversations around me. And not only were there conversations that I wanted to interpret, here was a different culture I wanted to understand as well.

When I finally landed back at Mascot airport, I was a very different person to the one who had set off on his own six weeks before. This might not have been immediately apparent, but in my own mind I had matured. When I had departed I was a casual cricketer and a boy from the Eastern Suburbs. Now I was a cricketer with a serious eye on the big-time . . . and a novice explorer with ambitions to see the world.

•CHAPTER 22•

'Bit Cold, Wasn't It?'

As soon as I could manage it after returning from my adventures with the Randwick Wanderers, I was out of the country again. I grabbed a quick flight to the Philippines with a couple of work-mates, and not long afterward had a fantastic time skiing in New Zealand, at Coronet Peak. One thing I will never forget about that particular visit to the Shaky Isles was a very brief swim I had in a very, very, very cold body of water called Lake Wakatipu. This was one of the most stupid things I have ever done in my life.

One of the group who travelled with us was a guy called Jim Tuite, who was the trainer with the Balmain rugby league club for many years. Jimmy was a fitness fanatic. So was I, as I saw peak fitness as one of the keys to fulfilling my ambitions on the cricket field. So, while the rest of the boys were venturing to the nearest bar and bistro after a day on the Coronet Peak ski-slopes, I would join Jim for a run. Anything to get that little bit fitter.

The chalet we were staying in was right on the lake . . . Lake Wakatipu. As we set off on our run each evening, the rest of the boys were up on the first-floor balcony, beers in hand, to cheer us on our way. We ran up the road that leads out of the village, along the side of an icy mountain stream and down a couple of dirt tracks before making it back to our starting point. When we returned, the boys were still there on the balcony, about two beers less sober than when we had begun, but still prepared to give us a rousing cheer as we recuperated near the chalet entrance.

For the first couple of nights, I headed up to my room for a quick shower and then joined our mates at the bar. But on the third evening Jimmy had other ideas. Out of the blue he suddenly announced: 'We've gotta go for a swim in this lake.'

You must remember this is the middle of winter. As quietly and politely as I could I commented: 'You've got to be fucking joking!!'

'No,' he continued, 'we're going to tough it out. It'll be good for your character.'

Basically, he humiliated me into it. Apparently this was one of the sacrifices I had to make if I wanted to make it to the top, although I couldn't quite see it that way. I wondered how many times Alan Davidson had swum across a frozen lake before he made it to the top of world cricket. And I tried to picture Dougie Walters stubbing out a cigarette before setting out for a half-hour paddle in the Arctic Ocean.

We went upstairs to put on our Speedos. This in itself was ridiculous. On went the Speedos, then the t-shirt, then the second t-shirt, the tracksuit pants, the four pairs of socks, the boots, sloppy joe, windcheater, three woollen jumpers, balaclava, gloves, beanie, scarf and waterproof jacket. Then Jim and I walked to the water's edge, and took all but the Speedos off again.

When we had set off for our run we had just a team of three out on the balcony to give us a cheer. Not now. Word had travelled fast. By now every single person staying at the Alpine village — guests and staff — were out there waiting to see us take our first step into the unknown.

I took my first step, and right then I realised what a complete bloody fool I was. It was liquid ice. I looked at Jim, and he was poised for his dive. So I, faithful servant that I was, took the plunge too and set out on the quickest 50 metres of freestyle I will ever swim in my life.

My body was screaming out for mercy and when I reached a point where I thought I had done my best, I turned around and swam back to the safety of the shore. Not for one moment was I game to stop, because I knew if I did I would have frozen on the spot. It was unbelievably painful — a lesson that taught me that freezing to death in ice-cold water must be the most horrendous death of all. When I reached dry land, I looked back and there was Jimmy, still swimming, about 150 metres away. How he got that far is something I will never know.

I quickly towelled down, put all of my gear on and then waited for him to return, which he eventually did. When he

finally strolled from the water, he glanced up at me with a look that was about half admiration for the fact that I'd had a go, and half disgust because I'd got out of there as quickly as I had. And then he winked at me, smiled, and said . . .

'Bit cold, wasn't it?'

•CHAPTER 23•

Seeing the World

One country that had a profound impact on me when I travelled there was the land of the Pharaohs — Egypt. The thing I found so hard to grasp about Egypt was the fact that, quite clearly, the society that existed way back when they were building miracles like the Great Pyramids and The Sphinx was extremely significant and ordered. But where did these extra-ordinary, sophisticated people go? How can something so triumphant and powerful disappear into the dust?

The Egypt of today is far different to the great civilisation of centuries past. But the landmarks that remain are testimony to the culture and grandeur of yesteryear. I walked into tombs that were thousands of years old, and the walls were as smooth as silk, all fashioned by hand. There were the astonishing hieroglyphics delicately painted on the wall and, of course, great wonders of the ancient world, constructed over many years, using manual labour and precise engineering. You could achieve these things today, sure, but you'd want the very latest in technology available before commencing work.

The other thing that blew me away was the heat! I kept thinking, how the hell could these people have worked in these conditions? . . . when their job was to be part of a team hauling a massive stone about 10 kilometres from the brickyard to the building site. The Valley of the Kings, near Luxor in Egypt, would have to be the hottest place on earth. Maybe Colombo in Sri Lanka might beat it for discomfort — the humidity there is the killer — but for pure, dry, oppressive heat, nothing in my travels has got near Egypt.

From Luxor we sailed down the Nile to the Aswan Dam, in a little sailing boat, a felucca, a type of ancient boat which has been cruising down the mighty river for hundreds of years. This was a fantastic, if time-consuming, experience, a million miles from the pace and stress of the 20th century. Our captain was a 60-plus-year-old Muslim who'd been doing the trip for all his life (he had two boat-boys for crew) and he took six days to get us to our destination. The pace of the journey was best summed up by the sight of the 'Cairo Princess' ferry, which held 200 people, churning its way past us one morning on its way to the Dam. Later that day, we struck the ferry again — on her way back. We hadn't got halfway there yet. But our mode of transport was so relaxing. And I wondered if the skipper of the Cairo Princess would have let me throw a fishing line over the side of his ship. I don't think so, which meant I wouldn't have caught a very succulent catfish I cooked for dinner on one of those six nights we spent sailing down the Nile.

Every evening, we'd stop for a break, before setting off again the next morning. At one pitstop, I took the time to clean my gear, which meant washing each item by hand, and then laying the lot out on the rocks to dry near the river's edge. At one point I was distracted by one of the boat-boys and when I turned back I saw a young local boy running off with part of my wardrobe. I took off after him, wearing no more than my Speedos, but didn't catch him until he'd made it back into the middle of the village where he lived.

He was only a very scared kid, and after I had made it plain I was more than a little cheesed off with what he had done, I let him keep the clothes. I gave him a gentle clip over the ear,

132

sent him on his way, and then turned to return to the felucca. It was about now that I realised this was a very devout Muslim village I was bang in the middle of. Not one person, male or female, had any flesh showing at all, except for M. Whitney, who was clad in nothing more than what had suddenly become a very brief pair of Speedos. All I could do was give it my best Crocodile Mick Dundee cheesy grin, and walk as quickly as I possibly could for the seclusion of my little boat.

After we had visited the enormous Aswan Dam, we decided to catch a train back to Cairo, a 20-hour-plus journey and an experience in itself. By the time we arrived at the station there wasn't a single first-class ticket to spare, which was an ugly problem because on the Aswan Dam-to-Cairo overnight train first-class meant okay and any class below that meant not okay. But we didn't want to hang around any longer, so we took the second-class tickets.

The first thing to be learned was that just because you had a ticket, there was no guarantee of a seat. On the contrary, by the time we jumped on board even the aisles, the conductor's cabin and the luggage racks were taken. It was absolutely jam-packed, with men, women, boys, girls, baggage, pets, chickens and various other animals fighting for a vantage point. And the atmosphere was horrible, over 40 degrees Celsius in the middle of the night, and putrid — about what you'd get if you mixed a sauna with an abattoir. We doubted the train had ever been cleaned in its life. And it had lived a long life.

I was travelling with six other guys — five Australians and a Kiwi, and we were the only white men on the entire train. Consequently, because of our appearance and our (relative) aura of opulence, the other occupants saw us as some kind of weird circus act. We planted ourselves near the doors that opened out from the middle of one of the carriages, with our back-packs rammed against those doors, and throughout the trip a collection of locals and African and Asian travellers took turns to barge though the crowd to catch a look at us. All we were doing was standing there, fighting to preserve our millimetre of territory, but the fact that our faces, skin, hair and language were so different was a source of great curiosity to them.

The train was absolutely chock-a-block, but when we reached the next station, it looked like half of Africa was waiting to get on board. One of the guys I was with was a big, big boy and he leaned over to 'our' door and, Schwarzenegger-like, grabbed the handle and refused to let go, despite the best efforts of the mob outside. We just stood there and laughed, as a succession, and then combinations, of tiny little Egyptians fought gallantly but unsuccessfully to open the door. When those stranded outside grew more desperate and started banging and kicking at the door, our comrade had to seek reinforcements, so that by the time the train departed there were three or four of us keeping the door locked shut, while the flock of locals left on the platform either aimed a perilous dive at another entry point, or began to make plans for an assault on the next train, which probably wasn't due until the following day.

This was just the first of a series of such battles. It must have been Grand Final day in Cairo, so huge were the waiting lists at each station, so at every stop (and there were plenty of them) until we finally reached our destination we manned the barriers, otherwise our little piece of territory would have been overrun.

From Cairo we travelled to Israel. There, an experience I'll never forget was in crossing the border between Egypt and Israel, at a time when relations between the two countries were at their most fragile. The interrogation I received from the Israeli guards went something like this:

'Where have you been?'

'I've been to Cairo, Luxor, Pyramids, down the Nile, back to Cairo . . .'

'Do you know anyone in Egypt?'

'No.'

'These your bags?'

'Yeah.'

'And you packed them?'

'Yep.'

'You don't know anyone in Egypt at all?'

'No.'

'And you are sure these are your bags?'

'Yeah. I'm sure.'

'Where's your passport.'

'Right here.'

'Are you Michael Roy Whitney?'

'Yes.'

'And these are your bags?'

'Yes, sir.'

'And you don't know anyone in Egypt?'

'I've already said . . .'

'If I opened these bags, you would know everything that is in them?'

'Yes, sir.'

'You're not carrying any gifts?'

'Oh yeah, I've bought some presents . . .'

With that he grabbed the bag, and tipped the contents out in front of me. The fact the presents were for my family at home, not items presented to me, was of no matter. He gave the bag and its contents the full going-over, leaving absolutely nothing to chance. And then he asked again:

'Are you sure you don't know anyone in Egypt?'

'Mate,' I said, 'I don't know a single bloody person in Africa! I'm an Australian and I'm on holidays.'

The guard looked up at me. He didn't apologise, smile or look at all sympathetic.

'We're just making sure,' was all he said.

Then he let me through. I wasn't angry with the guy — I knew he was just doing his job and that that job was a very difficult one. But I was dirty that relations between people can

degenerate to the point where such an exchange becomes a way of life.

The highlight of my time in Israel was a visit to the old city of Jerusalem. There is so much history, right from the moment you walk through the gates. Now, I'm not a really religious person, but for many years I've had a lot of questions about the concept of religion in my mind. I was brought up a Roman Catholic, and have a basic understanding of the principles of Christianity, but from my late teens I began questioning the things I had been taught: 'Hang on, this can't be right,' I'd say to myself. 'They're telling me all these things about this bloke who's supposed to be the number one, but there are all these people starving and being killed for no purpose. And most of the world's wars are about conflicts between religions.'

It just seemed to me that, if God was as almighty as He was

reputed to be, then why didn't He use that power to make the world a happier and more just place?

Jerusalem is arguably the most spiritual place on Earth. It is also one of the most fragmented. For Muslims, Jews and Christians it is a centre of great significance, with each belief seeing different sites in the old city as sacred. The first of these landmarks we visited was the Church of the Holy Sepulchre, which is situated at Golgotha, or Calvary, where Jesus Christ was crucified. Having been taught the Christian story as a kid, I was totally overwhelmed by the place. It was not that history was being played out before me, but here was a succession of landmarks, each playing an important part in the story of Christ's death and resurrection. Just metres from where the cross had been positioned is the rock on which it is said Jesus' body was placed after he was taken down from the cross. A few more metres further on is the tomb. While for me the encounter was not a particularly religious one, I couldn't help but notice how special an experience this was for many of those around me. These people had travelled from all parts of the world to be there and I truly admired their faith. But I also couldn't help thinking that they had made such an effort of faith without really knowing whether the bloke actually existed. That to me will always be one of life's great mysteries.

I will never forget the reaction of a group of nuns who were in front of me in a queue awaiting their turn at the place where the cross was hammered into the ground. They bent down and touched beneath the altar that marked the spot, and then reacted as if hit by a lightning bolt. A few seconds later I tried the same thing . . . but nothing happened.

A short walk from the Church of the Holy Sepulchre, through some narrow alleys, is the Dome of the Rock — the third holiest Muslim site on Earth after the Ka'ba in Mecca and the Mosque of the Prophet in Medina. According to tradition, the Dome of the Rock is the site from which God took Mohammad on his mystical night journey into heaven. In so many ways, it didn't seem right that such a holy place for Muslims could be so close to such a holy place for Christians. I mean, the two religions haven't exactly been the best of mates through the centuries. Then, to make matters even stranger, another 150 metres walk through the alleys of the Old City is the 18-metre Western Wall — for those of the Jewish faith the holiest site in the city. The Wall is the largest section still standing of four retaining walls that were built in 20BC to reinforce the Temple that had originally been constructed nearly 500 years before. That was the second Temple built on the site. The first had been built by King Solomon in the 10th century BC, but then obliterated by Nebuchadnezzar, the ruler of Babylon, in 587BC.

Again, the thing that hit me hardest was the sincerity and passion of those to whom the Wall meant a great deal. The Wall has, over the years, been referred to rather questionably as the 'Wailing Wall', in reference to the Jews who travel there to mourn the destruction of the first and second Temples. It has also been seen by Jews as some sort of communication link with God, and a most intriguing sight there is to see people scribbling messages onto pieces of paper and poking the messages into cracks in the Wall.

As I walked away from the Western Wall, I kept asking myself what had the Jews done through history that had made them such marked people. They are no more and no less fair dinkum about their faith than any other religion, yet they have been ridiculed and abused by others in some quite horrendous and appalling ways. That's what I cannot relate to in religion — the way one group of believers seems to think it has the right to hold and foster deep-seated hatreds of others. What gives one section of society the right to deplore and denounce another?

I often asked myself this question when I travelled to South Africa in 1984. I had met some South Africans on my Kontiki tour of Europe in 1982, and had become somewhat attached

to one lady in particular. For the two years after when we had gone our separate ways in '82 we had kept in touch through the telephone and the post office. Then, in 1984 I decided I would check the place out for myself and at the same time see if there was anything long-term in our fledgling relationship.

I also had a further motive. This was the period when a rebel Aussie cricket tour of South Africa was being organised. Back in the English summer of 1983, while I was playing league cricket for Littleborough, I had received an approach from the tour promoter, Bruce Francis, to see if I was interested. It was really hush-hush at the time, but we did reach the stage where he offered me $40,000 a year for two years to tour. For me, at that time, this was *humungous* money (though much less than what the players who did sign eventually received). However, the thought of taking any money at all to play in a country that seemed so justly reviled for its apartheid laws played on my conscience. I welcomed the opportunity to travel there and check things out for myself.

I did a tour of the country with my friend, and two of her friends from university, and although I was shielded (whether unwittingly or deliberately, I'm not sure) from the worst of the reality of apartheid, I still saw some ugly examples of how the laws preserved the white's dominance. One day in Pretoria, I saw a policeman pull a whip on three or four blacks who had made the mistake of congregating on a street corner. That, according to the law, was illegal.

The conditions the blacks lived under at that time were dreadful, and left a bad taste in my mouth. Not only that, the attitude the whites had towards the blacks appalled me as well. Unfortunately, my friend was as bad as any of them. She was, purely and simply, a racist. Whenever I began to put my view on the situation, she would come back with: 'You don't live here. You don't understand.' I had gone over there with visions of changing the world, but within a week I was doing no more than keeping my mouth shut. A large number of white South

Africans I met appeared so set in their ways, and so sure of their position, that for me to start talking of justice and change was to do no more than alienate myself from most of the people I knew there. The majority of whites appeared to have very little, if any, sympathy for the plight of the blacks.

Looking back, the thing I can't believe is that such people as Mandela and de Klerk were able to initiate the great reforms that occurred in the '90s. Having experienced the attitudes of many white South Africans in 1984, I would not have thought such a revolution was possible in so short a period of time.

Although its politics were cruel, South Africa remains one of the most beautiful countries on earth. Durban, where my lady friend lived, reminded me a lot of Sydney, with its beaches and its surf life. Kruger Park, the game reserve, was fantastic, Cape Town, and the majestic Table Mountain, as impressive as any

SOUTH AFRICA RUNNING BETWEEN WICKETS

post card has ever portrayed it. We travelled to Stellenbosch, which is famous for its wineries, but I can only remember up to lunchtime. We drove through the Karoo desert, and travelled the garden route, along the coast from Cape Town, to see some famous surfing beaches I had always wanted to visit.

We also travelled to Sun City, which simultaneously amazed and appalled me. To get there, you have to travel through Bophuthuswana, where everyone has nothing, but then suddenly huge billboards start appearing by the side of the road bearing their messages, 'Smoke Marlboro' or 'Five Miles to Sun City'. When we arrived, I was astonished by the opulence of the place. Here, in the middle of the desert and in a region otherwise dominated by poverty and misfortune, was a top-of-the-range 18-hole golf course and a series of casinos, restaurants, convention centres and six-star accommodation hotels.

I can't remember a single funny story to come out of my time in South Africa. For me, it was a country at that time that just did not lend itself to humour. As for that girl from Durban: we had written to each other and called each other regularly in the two years since the Kontiki trip and had spent five weeks together seeing as much of the country as we could. But from the time I kissed her on the cheek and boarded the plane that took me on to England I have not spoken or written to her. Nor she to me. I think we both realised our views on the world were just too far apart.

It was on that flight to London that I decided that, no matter how much money Bruce Francis offered, I was not going to accept a spot in his rebel team. Perhaps you might think it easy for me to sit here today and say that, because the fact is, I missed the entire 1984–85 season and wasn't a candidate for the side anyway. But I know in my heart I wouldn't have gone. Having seen the place in 1984 I simply couldn't have.

South Africa, of course, was not the only country in the world with massive inequalities between rich and poor. One of the first overseas countries I ever visited was the Philippines, to where, in the days when my workmates at Qantas and I could snatch cheap flights, I would head at regular intervals for a few days at the coastal resorts. Our haven there was a place called Olongapo City.

I remember on one of our visits we were joined by a large proportion of the US Navy, who had just sailed into nearby Subic Bay, America's huge naval base in the Philippines, aboard one of Uncle Sam's biggest aircraft carriers. In one fell swoop, more than 5000 of the US Navy's finest invaded the local area. With them came a succession of fights, between Americans and Americans and Americans and locals, and each time the local US Military Police were quickly in amongst them, piling the bloodied combatants into their jeeps for a quick trip back to base.

It was at Olongapo City that I witnessed one of the most insane events I ever saw in my life — the mayhem and cruelty of an organised cock fight. After paying a tiny amount to get in, we sat in stands about 15 rows deep and watched a series of contests. What was most bizarre for me was the sight of people placing wagers on the bouts — blokes were betting between themselves and there were bookies operating down the front. And when the fight was over, each wager was settled, with blokes pointing up into the stand before bills were passed down from the people in the back rows who had done their money.

We only stayed for three or four fights. Once the novelty wore off we saw the thing for what it was — a very, very ugly show.

I was shocked by the poverty of the areas we travelled through to get to Olongapo City. The City itself was a resort for westerners, complete with most of the comforts of modern living. But away from the nightlife and the gourmet restaurants were areas of squalor and decay. This was a culture far from the world I grew up in and I set out to have a close and genuine look. Simple things, such as a massive rice field featuring hundreds of employees working without any modern machinery, struck a chord with me. I went looking for the 'other' side, and tried to gain an appreciation of how the people who lived under such hardship could enjoy and gain satisfaction from their lives.

That same curiosity was the reason I travelled to the mountains of Kashmir in India during an adventure in 1984. By the time I reached Kashmir I had been on the move for quite a while, to places as contrasting as South Africa, England, Greece and Eastern Europe. India was something very different again.

I had met up with four other friends from Sydney. I had met up with one couple, Greg and Karen Charlwood, in Bombay, and from there the three of us had caught a train to New Delhi where we picked up Tony and Mary White, who were on their honeymoon. This was Mary's first time out of Australia. Not a bad place to start, I reckon — from Pagewood in Sydney's

eastern suburbs to the north of India! From Delhi we flew to Srinagar, where we stayed on a houseboat at a place called Dahl Lake.

To climb into the mountains near the Pakistani border we had to catch a bus to a village called Gulmag, which means 'valley of the flowers'. It is a truly beautiful place. My first impression of Gulmag came on arrival; a semi-circle of wooden huts, about 150 metres long. We had stopped just about in the centre of that semi-circle. As we came in, people came charging from the huts, which were all shops, cheering and yelling and slapping the side of the bus. At first we were apprehensive, but not for long, as we noticed the huge smiles on the faces of our 'attackers'. It turned out, the bus only arrived once every three days and the locals were overjoyed, as its arrival meant on the one hand, fresh supplies, and on the other, customers to buy their wares.

Our ambition was to climb a mountain called 'Alpatha', of around 6000 metres. We went looking for a local guide, and the best we could find was a little old bloke who seemed at least 75. This, we thought, might be a problem, as the slope we were aiming at was more vertical than horizontal and we'd been told the climb would take seven and a half hours to complete — four to get up, three and a half to get back down. However the old guy assured us he was the best there was . . . and at nine the next morning, off we went.

The first hour of the trip involved a 'gentle' climb on what was, compared with what lay ahead, no more than a slight incline. It was a sort of calm before the storm. By the time the mountain started to get steeper, the girls were struggling and asked if we could take time out at a little hut, inside which was an old fella who offered us a cup of tea and a simple meal. Far better than the food and drink was the awesome view the hut offered of the mountains.

We offered Karen and Mary the option: 'If you don't want to climb the mountain you can hang around here all day and wait for us.' They stared up at the climb ahead of us, had a quick glance at the breathtaking view they'd be obliged to admire all day, took another gulp out of their coffee, looked at each other, grinned and said: 'That's cool.'

So away we went, the four of us, on the steepest part of the climb. After an hour we looked up and it seemed we'd made no headway at all. The going was slow and the air was getting thinner all the time. We needed a break, so we yelled out to our veteran guide up ahead of us that we wanted to call a time-out. He just waved his hand, and stopped. And then he did a most remarkable thing. He searched the area immediately around him, found a spot to his liking, lay down on the ground, and went straight to sleep.

Twenty minutes later, we gave him a nudge. He bounced up, and off we went. After another hour we had to stop again, and the process was repeated. He crashed again . . . instantly. From talking to the old guy, we discovered he did this climb twice a week, without a problem. Although the pit-stops became more frequent the higher we went, we eventually reached the summit to savour a view the equal of anything I will ever see in my life.

On the far side was a valley, which was dominated by a part-frozen lake. Half the lake was frozen over, the other half was a fantastic vivid blue, with icebergs littered across its surface. The lake's edge appeared to be no more than a 10-minute walk down a reasonably-defined track. 'We've got to go and have a look at this,' we said to each other. And we did, even though our guide seemed to have some concerns. When we reached the edge of the lake, but not until after we'd been totally blown away by the beauty of the scene before us, we noticed that the path continued down beyond the lake further into the valley. We were keen to see what was down there, but at this point our guide stepped in and said firmly: 'Not to go.' He told us that the area was a demarcation zone between Kashmir and Pakistan, and it wasn't safe to enter. There was always the chance that one or other of the two sides might drop something explosive into the vicinity.

A second journey out of Gulmag took us to the Kolahoi Glacier, which was an unbelievable piece of terrain. Almost as amazing was a chicken meal we enjoyed along the way. We were heading up the side of a mountain, towards the glacier, when we came upon a hut on the side of the track, with smoke puffing out of a chimney. Beside the hut was a multi-coloured tent.

The hut was part home, part shop; located there for the trekkers who passed by. The guy who ran the place was quick to offer a meal and a drink. 'Apple goose' was his speciality, which I quickly realised was in fact apple juice. And he suggested we try his barbecued chicken. I followed the guy out the back — to his backyard, which was also home for about 30 chickens. He had a big knife tucked hidden behind his back. As soon as he arrived, the chooks tried to take off . . . it was very obvious they were aware someone else had ordered the roast chicken. Unfortunately for them there was no escape; the chef quickly cornered one poor bird and in one sweep sliced off its head. From there he moved to the fire, to cook up what was, and still is, the best barbecued chicken I have ever eaten.

We pitched our tent there and stayed for two days. During our stay we became involved in a game of cricket with a group of locals. Even in the mountains, the people of India love their cricket. At one point, Tony mentioned to the chef that I had played cricket for Australia, which was obviously exciting to him, if only because that meant I had met his cricket hero . . . 'King' Hughes. I suggested the guy's name was 'Kim' not 'King', but apparently I was mistaken. It was definitely King Hughes, and no amount of argument from me was going to change the fellow's mind.

The Kolahoi Glacier when we eventually reached it was absolutely awesome. It is one of those very rare creations of nature that is hard to believe, even if you're right there looking at it. Half of the glacial plain is rock and rubble, where the glacier had once been, the rest is just this fantastic 'river' of ice that appears to be immobile but is in fact creeping down the mountain. On either side of the plain are the mountain walls, going up to more than 6000 metres. The feeling of smallness and humility you get when you look up at the stark valley walls where the glacier has gouged a path out of the mountain range is something that will always stay with me. You really feel a minute, insignificant part of this remarkable world.

India had a profound effect on me and on my ideas about humanity. I had been to a lot of places before I journeyed there but, from the moment I first arrived, I thought: 'Wow, this is another planet!' The people were so different to any I had ever known. To many Indians, Australia was not a country so much as a team that played cricket. I would explain that I was from Australia and they would look at me like a six-month child who hasn't yet learned to talk. But if I discussed Australia in terms of cricket we were suddenly on the same wavelength. It was bizarre, as if cricket was their one link with the rest of the world.

The country has everything — every emotion, every smell, every colour. It has wealth, but the impact of the ruling class was for me totally swept away by the striking examples of poverty that are so evident. Despite their difficult existence and their sparse resources, I found the people to be, like the majestic terrain of Kashmir and South Africa, the sacred sites of Jerusalem and the remarkable relics of Ancient Egypt, fantastic and inspiring. To me the same is true of the workers on the rice fields near Olongapo City in the Philippines, and the men, women and children who were for so many years confined to the homelands and townships in South Africa. I will never cease to be amazed by the brave way these people battle on, despite their hardships, fashioning lives both rewarding and worthwhile.

•CHAPTER 24•

Battling Bulgarians and Checkpoint Charlie

By 1982, I'd had a gutful of Qantas, especially so over hassles concerning the issue of time off for cricket. I had one overseas flight due to me, so I resigned and flew to England. First stop was Fleetwood, where I'd played league cricket in '81. Then, as so many other young wide-eyed Aussies have done before and since, I set off on a Kontiki tour of Europe. Afterwards I met up with one of my best mate's elder brothers, Al, and his girlfriend, and flew to Greece. Unlike most tourists, who head for the beautiful islands, we drove through the middle of the country in a Kombi van with another couple Al had known in London. This part of Greece was stunning to look at and fascinating to experience.

Chance is a funny thing. The three of us were drinking one day on the verandah of a bar, within view of where a ferry unloaded its passengers and their vehicles. Off came this Kombi, which Al immediately recognised. We ran down to say G'day and eventually decided to team up with the other couple for the drive through Europe.

From Greece we headed for Istanbul in Turkey and then on beyond the Iron Curtain . . . to Hungary, Yugoslavia, Bulgaria, hopped to the western world in Austria, then East Germany and Berlin, on through Germany, then by boat to Copenhagen, another boat to Sweden and finally ended up in Stockholm. It was there that I saw The Steve Miller Band live, which in itself was a buzz, if mainly for the way the crowd, most of whom couldn't understand a word the band sang or said, would only jump and dance and sing when they heard a song they knew. By contrast, we (and by 'we' I mean a large number of travelling Aussies, Americans and Poms who had congregated in the same area, near the stage) went crazy for the entire show. We stood out like polar bears in a desert.

The ways of Eastern Europe at that time were an eye-opener. I remember in Bulgaria, Al's mate discovered a foolproof way of making a few dollars. He found out that if you were a tourist from outside Bulgaria and you exchanged US dollars for the local currency, you received eight times the normal exchange rate. Because of the parlous state of the Bulgarian economy, US dollars were looked upon as being akin to gold. Such a fiscal philosophy seemed like manna from heaven to a poor tourist such as our travelling comrade, who devised a strategy that involved exchanging as many US dollars as he could and then hanging on to all the local stuff he didn't spend until we reached Austria, where he would turn them back into US dollars and make a killing.

He was begging us to get into his scheme, which we all did to various extents. But he went all the way, and handed over US$200 to a disbelieving Sofia bank clerk. In return he received the biggest wad of banknotes seen in the entire history of Bulgaria. And though he set out to spend as much of it as he could, he was still in a position, according to his own calculations, to a make a very handsome profit when we arrived in Vienna.

Eventually it was time to leave Bulgaria and we arrived at the border control, where we were asked to step out of our Kombi. We faced the usual interrogation — nothing too sinister — until one of the border guards asked the magic question . . .

'Have any of you any currency you want to declare?'

'Ah, what exactly do you mean?'

'Do any of you have any Bulgarian currency with you?'

We had to put our hands up. I volunteered that I had about US$20 worth, Al had about the same, while our financial whiz still had enough bills to wallpaper a three-storey house.

'It is illegal to take Bulgarian currency out of Bulgaria,' the guard declared. 'You will have to leave all that with us.'

'What do you mean . . . leave it with you?'

The glare from beneath this border guard's army cap explained *exactly* what he meant.

Our colleague had just blown the best part of US$200, which for a tourist travelling on a very tight budget was a total disaster. And there was nothing any of us could do about it.

MIKE WHITNEY CONFRONTS CHECKPOINT CHARLIE

No-one had told us we couldn't take currency out of the country, and it was way too late to do anything about it now.

We had another discouraging experience in East Berlin. It was 1984 — more than five years before the Wall came down. To get from West Berlin to East Berlin involved going through the infamous Checkpoint Charlie. I remember a museum there, called 'The Wall', on the West Berlin side, which served as a memorial to those who had tried to cross the Wall to the West. This is the sort of place that can really slow you down for a while, as you ponder the hardship some people have had to live with through their lives, and reflect on the courage they needed to face that hardship. One 'exhibit' in that museum lives in my mind with me forever — a car, with a fuel tank modified so there was one compartment in the tank for the petrol and another for a man or woman to hide.

We spent a day in East Berlin and before we returned through Checkpoint Charlie we found a restaurant no more than 200 metres from the crossover where we decided to spend what was left of our East German currency. No-one had to tell us we wouldn't be able to take it back to West Berlin! However, spending the cash wasn't easy, as everything was so cheap. But we tried our best, buying more than a couple of rounds of drinks.

I was so paranoid about my wallet and passport that I sat on them for every second we were in that place. Unfortunately, Al wasn't quite so careful, and left his bag next to his chair. After we paid the bill (and left an absolute monster of a tip), he stood up and headed for the gents. We sat there a minute longer waiting for him to get back. When he returned the first thing he noticed was that his bag was missing!

'Stand at the door!' Al yelled at me, and I jumped up to play the role of bouncer. I wasn't letting anyone out. His wallet, money, passport, everything was in that bag. Everyone in the restaurant froze, like innocent customers in a bank during a robbery — in fact, it could well have appeared as though we were holding the joint up. Al looked around for a second, sized the situation up, and charged for the kitchen. In the time he'd been away he reckoned the only people who could have pinched his property were the staff who'd been walking around the restaurant. And he was right — as he got to the kitchen door, one of the waitresses appeared with the bag and a rather pathetic explanation that one of the staff had picked it up because they thought someone had left it behind.

A few people got up to leave. 'No-one's goin' anywhere yet,' Al roared, as he tipped the contents of his bag out on a table. Fortunately, everything was there, and after he repacked every-thing away he looked up, grinned for the first time in a few minutes, and announced in his best friendly police sergeant voice: 'Everything's fine now, ladies and gentlemen. You are all free to go.'

With that, even though at least 95 per cent of the people in the restaurant couldn't speak a word of English, most bolted for the door. The least I could do, having manned the door in a very aggressive manner throughout the ordeal, was to wish everyone a nice day as they departed.

We weren't keen about staying too long either and, as quickly as we could without breaking into a run, we set off for Checkpoint Charlie. The crossover back to the free world wasn't a problem, and once we'd made it through I suggested to Al that he recheck his bag, just to make sure nothing was missing. The money was all there, as were the travellers' cheques, and his passport. But as he flicked through his passport he stopped on the page where his photo was glued in. Something wasn't right. He gave the page a bit of a shake . . . and the photo fell out. Whoever had taken his bag had searched for and found the passport, turned to the right page, and begun to cut Al's photo out. A few more seconds and it would have been gone; a few more seconds after that, we assumed, and a substitute photo would have been there in its place. A few more minutes and someone would have been trying to con the guards at

Checkpoint Charlie. What Al would have been doing if all this had happened, we didn't like to speculate.

The realisation of what had occurred, and the ramifications had Al not figured out so quickly where his bag had gone, were a stark testimony to the desperate way of life for many of the residents of East Berlin of that time. Five years later, when the dreaded Berlin Wall finally came down, the first people I thought of were the men and women who worked in that restaurant. Hopefully, the stresses of life behind the Iron Curtain had been eased at least a little.

•CHAPTER 25•

African Adventure

No matter to where or when I've travelled, every time I return to Australia I always feel I'm coming back to the best country on earth. It's fabulous to have the chance to visit other places in the world, but we really do live in the equivalent of the Garden of Eden. We have opportunity here. If you work hard you can be rewarded. In other countries you don't always have that opportunity.

In the Australian winter of 1987, I set off on another expedition around the world. The big difference this time was that I was travelling with the lady who was to become my wife. I had first met Debbie on New Year's Eve, 1982, but it wasn't until 1986 that we really became fair dinkum about our relationship. In '87, our journey began in the United States, before we travelled to England and then into the heart of Africa, to Kenya, Tanzania and Zimbabwe.

America was a wild, occasionally scary, sometimes beautiful, often amazing adventure. My starkest memories are of incidents such as one we experienced one night in New Orleans, when Debbie was grabbed by a guy outside a shopfront. Deb was about 10 metres away from me when it happened, and the guy thought she was on her own. All I yelled out was 'HEY!! . . .' and he froze, let Deb go, and screamed out:

'Don't shoot me! Don't shoot me, master!! Please . . . don't shoot me!'

Then he ran, and I guess for every centimetre until he was out of sight he fully expected a bullet in his back.

That was seven years ago. Heaven knows how much worse it is today.

Before reaching New Orleans, we drove around Colorado, which is one of the most beautiful places on earth, far and away from the hustle, bustle and 21st century pressures of the big cities that most people picture when they think of America. Some of the relics of the Native American way of life we saw there were as remarkable as anything I had seen in Egypt.

New York City had a profound effect on me too. I really loved Manhattan. One of the first things I did after we arrived there was check out John Lennon's house. Lennon was one of my first heroes, and I can still remember feeling totally devastated on that day in 1980 when he was assassinated. Afterwards, I walked through Central Park, went down to the Statue of Liberty, and took in Wall Street, the Empire State Building, Broadway, and so much more.

I also got a buzz out of Chicago, especially an afternoon at the baseball at famous Wrigley Field, for a Cubs–Cincinnati Reds game. The first thing that knocked me over came well before the first pitch. I walked through the turnstile and a bloke handed me an umbrella. It was 'Umbrella Day', I was told, which meant the first 5000 people through the gate received an umbrella, complete with the logo of the Cubs and of the company who were sponsoring the promotion. I thought at the time (and still think): 'Why couldn't we do this sort of thing in Australian cricket?' In the program I noticed that at other times during the baseball season they have 'Cap Day', 'Mug Day' (as in things you drink out of), 'Pin Day' and so on.

What a great way to market the game. You can't go far

wrong giving the fans something for taking the time to come to the ground.

San Francisco — the cable cars, Alcatraz, the Golden Gate Bridge and the Bay — was super, and from there we drove down to Carmel, where Clint Eastwood was mayor. While we were there, we had a drink in the 'Dogbreath Cafe', which the great actor owns. The thing that stuck in my mind was the way every single patron in the joint would turn and look at the front door every time someone entered. I don't think there was one patron in the place who wasn't hoping the owner might pop in for a quick coffee or a beer.

I don't think I could live in America. For all the great things, great places and quality people, the undercurrent of violence that pervades their way of life, especially in the really big cities, is just too unattractive for me. In 1993, on my way to England to join the commentary team on that year's Ashes series, we spent two days in Los Angeles and all I did was look over my shoulder. I went to visit a friend in downtown LA and was genuinely terrified as I tried to find his address. No-one should have to live that way, yet for many young people in urban America, that is their only choice.

Before we arrived in Kenya in '87, the picture I had in my head about the place was from the old movies and TV shows that used to portray a British colony, circa 1870, complete with game hunters who wore safari suits and pith helmets and had the melons of their greatest hunting conquests mounted on the walls of their stately homes. Yet the first thing I noticed when we landed in Nairobi was that 99.9 per cent of the people there were not British at all, but small Africans. Being over 180cm tall and a white Australian, I stood out like Curtly Ambrose in a Sydney pre-school playground.

Like just about every tourist who makes it to Kenya, we were keen to see the game parks, through a camping tour. So we set out to discover a reputable firm to take us where we wanted to go. Finding a company available to do the job wasn't difficult at all — there were hundreds of them. The problem was working out the right one. All we had to do was walk down Nairobi's main street looking like tourists and within seconds we were inundated by hosts of salesmen simultaneously recommending their product and denouncing their competition. The companies represented had all sorts of exotic African names — from 'Serengeti Plains Tours', 'Lake Nakura Safaris' and 'Masai Mara Treks' to many we couldn't pronounce or understand.

But one mob stood out. While most of the salesmen were jabbering away or even physically trying to shoulder us towards their sales office, one guy just meandered over, handed us his promotional leaflet and then walked away. I had a quick look at the leaflet, and was knocked over by the name of his company . . .

'Best Camping'.

Just that, pure and simple. Not long afterward, we saw the extremely humble 'Best Camping' head office, complete with table, two chairs, filing cabinet, map of Africa on the wall and not much else. Within five minutes we'd booked our adventure. One of their bus tours was leaving the next day, and it seemed exactly what we wanted. The only thing that worried us was the unimaginative company name.

As it turned out, the only thing 'Best Camping' couldn't control was the weather. On our bus (which could have taken 15 passengers) were two people from Ireland, Fergal and Caroline (with who we were to spend a fair bit of time in Africa), a couple from France, a driver, a guide, Debbie and me.

We headed up into the Serengeti Plains and the Masai Mara (the game park on the Serengeti) to witness some of the most spectacular sights on this earth. The first sighting was of about 25 kilometres worth of wildebeest migrating across the landscape, in a massive cloud of dust, as they headed north. You couldn't call it a *herd* — it was so much more than that — but even so, our guide estimated that three weeks earlier there had been *three times* the number. I am not kidding, from horizon to horizon there was an ongoing rush of wildebeest.

It was extraordinary, but there was so much more. We saw a huge variety of other native animals, giraffes, kudus, lions, rhinos, cheetahs, hyenas. The only thing that disappointed me was the way the tourist dollar had obviously prostituted the scene to some extent. There were a great number of buses like ours out there, and more than once a situation developed where something exciting would be discovered by one bus, such as when we found a cheetah with her recently-born cubs, and within minutes, after the word had gone out on the radio, six or seven other buses had dashed for the spot and formed an awkward circle around the mother and her new family.

It seemed to me, just at that moment, that it wouldn't have been inappropriate for someone to race out and erect a circus tent over the animals. But I don't know what the solution to that is. Just like me, everyone else in every other bus wanted to see the cheetah and her babies in their natural environment. But what we were doing was imposing on that cheetah on her own turf. And in our own small way we were doing our bit towards ruining the natural environment.

What was fascinating was the manner in which the cheetah shielded her offspring from the intruders. I would have backed that mother to outpace any of the buses in a head-to-head sprint, but with her young by her side taking off was not an option. Instead, she piloted the kids into a strip of long grass that ran alongside a beaten track, and while she walked along the open path, the tiny cheetahs hid, out of view, in the grass. And if any of the little fellas tried to make it out onto the track, the mother let out with a hissing sound, and the young miscreant dived back in to where mother thought it was safe.

Camping is not allowed in the Masai Mara, so each night we pitched our tents just outside the game park boundary. Of course, the three or four other Best Camping buses on tour at

160

that time all camped at the same place, so the camping ground became a great place to meet people.

It was on our first night in the wild that Best Camping's inability to keep a hold on the weather proved disastrous. Their dinner fare had proved better than okay, and the tents were roomy, sturdy and hadn't taken much more than 30 seconds to put up. But just as we made plans to crash for the night, a flash of lightning lit up the horizon. And then another, and another. 'Happens all the time,' we were told by the guides. 'There's absolutely nothing to worry about.'

However, at about 2am, I was woken by a weird, floating feeling, and within seconds I realised I was lying in about six inches of water. Outside it was belting down at a million miles an hour. Then, as the ground around us swiftly changed to mud, the pegs that held the tent up began to give away. I jumped up

(and in the process gave Debbie a hefty whack in the jaw) and dashed outside to gallantly but unsuccessfully try and save our temporary home from collapse. More than one of our drenched comrades the next morning commented that the sight of Michael Roy Whitney, with not a stitch of clothing on, trying to keep his tent from caving in was not a particularly pretty sight.

To make matters worse, exactly the same thing happened again the next night, but this time fortunately I had taken the precaution of going to sleep wearing my jocks and a t-shirt.

Another thing I remember about sleeping overnight with Best Camping was waking the next morning and noticing animal tracks around the fire, the bus and the tents. Again, our trusty guide was unimpressed. 'Absolutely nothing to worry about,' he explained. 'Just hyenas.' The bastards had been in the campsite during the night, scrounging for scraps. We hadn't heard a thing. I wondered whether there had been vultures swooping overhead as well.

After our Best Camping tour was completed, we travelled south to Lake Nakuru, to see the flamingoes that have made the lake so famous. We then returned to Nairobi, to catch a train to Mombasa. From there we journeyed to two more game parks, Tsavo and Amboseli, primarily to see the elephants for which these places are renowned.

An incident occurred on that Nairobi–Mombasa train trip that reminds me strangely of a time in Adelaide when I had a dinner date with Greg Matthews. On this occasion, Mo was crooked that his steak wasn't cooked the way he'd requested and as he sent his order back to the kitchen, he let the waiter know about it.

I told him he was mad to do that. My father had worked for a while as a steward with the Merchant Navy in Australia, and he told me some horrific stories of what the cook used to do with the meals of the blokes who complained about what was coming from the kitchen. No ingredient or cooking technique was too crass if the whingeing was too heavy. It is something I have never forgotten. Consequently, I have never moaned about a restaurant meal. I just assume the guys and girls over the stove are already doing their best.

For all Greg knew, his complaints might have led to the chef throwing his steak to the kitchen floor before he jumped all over it. What might have been added to the mushroom sauce was anyone's guess. When the meal came back, Mo was as quiet as a number 11 facing Patrick Patterson. I don't think he enjoyed it all that much.

Dinner on the Nairobi to Mombasa train was served in two sittings. Fifty per cent of the passengers were fed between 5pm and 7pm, the other 50 per cent between 7pm and 9pm. The menu consisted of a choice between about three entrees, four main courses, two desserts and tea or coffee, which looked terrific on paper. We had heard that by the time the second session began, the choice had generally been whittled down to soup, chicken salad, ice cream and a communal tea bag.

Fergal was, for an Irishman, a pretty placid bloke. However, having heard about the advantages of being served early, he was very pushy about being part of the first session, to the point of abusing the chief waiter when it became apparent we'd been picked in the seconds. Then, taking things a step further, after he realised there was no way the allocations were going to change he was very adamant we were going to be the first table served on sitting number two.

I don't think the waiters would have been game to take anyone else's order before our Irish friend's, but even so, our asparagus soups took an eternity to arrive. Not just for us though, for throughout the carriage murmurs of complaint about the tardy service gradually grew. After about half an hour, Fergal had had enough.

'Where's my bloody soup?' he roared in his thick Dublin accent.

The chief waiter was a native African, a big fellow about 190cm tall, who looked like the basketballer Magic Johnson and didn't so much walk between tables, as lumber. As Fergal leered up at him and demanded to know where his entree was, the waiter didn't bat an eyelid. He just stared out towards the sunset and, when the tirade was over, calmly turned on his heel and walked back into the kitchen.

A little later, he was back with our soups. 'What you've got to do to get service around here,' Fergal muttered as 'Magic' placed our first course in front of us. But as we looked at our meals, we quickly realised that very likely Fergal's aggressive strategy hadn't been too shrewd. My father's philosophy had been proven true once more. For, while three of the soups were fine, Fergal's was a horrendous, sticky substance that you wouldn't have given to your worst enemy.

Or maybe you would? Fergal never bothered with the main course or dessert. And many times during our stay in the dining car we thought we could hear muffled laughter and the sound of native Kenyans trying their best to imitate angry Irish accents.

One of the strangest things I ever did on my various travels occurred on our last day in Nairobi. I bought a pot. Not just any pot, but a huge metre-and-a-half tall hand-crafted monster. It wasn't until after I'd parted with the cash and hauled the thing back to our hotel that I started to consider how it was going to get back to Australia. As a short-term solution, I carefully wrapped it in foam, and carried it onto the train to Mombasa. When we reached Mombasa I lugged it down to the post office, to see if there was any way I could get it posted back to Australia.

The guy behind the counter measured it up and said with a huge smile: 'If you get a box that it will fit in, I will post it for you.'

Fantastic. I'd developed a real affection for that pot, but I didn't like the idea of carrying it any further. Finding a box was a problem, however, and an extensive search of Mombasa failed to turn up what I was looking for. So I put the pot in storage, jotted the dimensions down on a piece of paper, and headed off

to an island called Lamu up the coast for a few days. I carried the dimensions with me because the island, as well as being a beautiful part of the world, was also a haven for wood carving. And sure enough, I found a carver who was able to build the box I needed, and I was a very happy pot owner when I returned to our base in Mombasa with a beautifully moulded plywood box perched on my shoulder.

The pot fitted like the proverbial glove and first thing the next morning I headed back to the post office to organise the transport back to Sydney. However, the post office employee I had spoken to before wasn't on duty; instead there was a big, fat bloke perched on a stool behind the counter.

'Excuse me, sir,' I said quietly. 'I'd like to post this box back to Sydney, Australia, please.'

'You can't,' he said in a deep, deep voice. He hadn't even looked at the thing.

'Why not?'

'Because I said so.'

He would have made a great cricket umpire.

'You have to sea freight,' he informed me.

'But that's not what the gentleman who was working here a couple of days ago said.'

'He not the boss. I the boss and you have to sea freight.'

'How much will that cost?'

'I do not know. We don't sea freight here.'

I looked at him, he looked at me, and then, right at that moment, I decided . . . bugger it, I'll get the bloody thing home myself.

One day, on the way back from the Masai Mara, we decided to visit a Masai village. The Masai people have lived in Kenya and Tanzania for centuries, and are the one being the King of the Jungle, the African lion, is genuinely scared of. It is a tradition that a Masai boy cannot become a warrior until he has actually killed a lion and, because over the years the Masais have developed heaps of warriors, it would seem the lions' fears are well-founded.

We pulled up outside a Masai village in Kenya, to be greeted by an amazing sight. The six-foot-something gentleman who came out to welcome us was a full-scale, fair-dinkum warrior, complete with no shoes, robe, hair plastered back by a mixture of ochre from the earth and cow fat, war paint over his face and body, spears, shield, the works. And I mean the works, because in his ear-lobe, was an empty Kodak film container. We assumed the earring was the guy's attempt at assimilating into western society. It was just about the most absurd thing I have ever seen in my entire life.

Then, as if to prove how much he knew about western society, we had to haggle over the entry fee before we could take a closer look at this centuries-old way of life. First up, he wanted US$50 each, then $20, then $10, then $20 for the four of us, which bought us entry and a guided tour through the village, into certain huts (but not the chief's — he was having a kip), and the cattle pen.

From Mombasa, we journeyed on to Zanzibar, where we stayed at the 'Old England' club. Zanzibar had once been a part of the British Empire, then been taken over by the Sultan of Oman before it became part of Tanzania. The rooms we stayed in were pretty threadbare, but parts of the joint had not been touched since the days when the Poms ruled the roost. There was a billiard room, complete with two 12 × 6 tables, that hadn't seen a cue lifted in anger in many decades. And there was a library, complete with a fairly extensive range of literature from the 19th century and the first 30-odd years of the 20th century. I went searching for the cricket section and found a few classics, including *Turn of the Wheel*, Percy Fender's story of the 1928–29 Ashes Tests in Australia (The Don's first Test series), and *In Quest of the Ashes*, Douglas Jardine's account of the acrimonious bodyline series. These were real collector's items, left unread for the best part of 30 or 40 years. If I'd pinched them, no-one would have known the difference, and I knew they would have looked real nice on my bookshelf at home.

One night in Zanzibar we strolled over to a travel agent's window, to see if there was any other place on the island we should check out. Suddenly, a bloke tapped me on the shoulder. 'Aren't you Mike Whitney?' he said. He was an Aussie bloke — 'Laurie from Queensland, and this is my girlfriend Sally' — and they explained how they had just rented a house on the other side of the island. Would we like to join them? 'That would be fantastic,' so Debbie and I went back to the Old England club, grabbed my pot, and set off for Laurie's place.

The house was located near a small fishing village called Twaka, which I will always remember for the market that came to life after the fishing boats returned from a morning out in the Indian Ocean. It was unbelievable — every seafood dish ever invented was available at this market, and at prices unheard of in Australia. Lobsters were on sale for less than you'd pay for a Big Mac at home.

After a day in the back stalls, Laurie and I decided that on day two we'd make a bid or two. But the prices were so outrageous (cheap!), and the tucker so attractive, we felt obliged to whack our hands up for just about everything. By the time we were finished we had fish, calamari, lobster, more fish, the works — heaps more than we needed and all bought for a song. In fact, we had so much seafood, my arms started to ache when we hauled the stuff back to our house. It was worse than carrying the pot.

We had only a few hundred more metres to go on the trip back to our house when, from nowhere, a local bloke appeared.

'I live here, in this house,' he said, pointing at the run-down little construction located right next to ours. 'I am a very good cook. I will cook your food for you. Which way you like?'

I looked at Laurie and Laurie looked at me. We were both

thinking exactly the same thing. This fella was trying to pinch our food.

'No thanks, mate. We'll be okay.'

'It is not what you think,' he continued. 'I am a very good man. I will cook the food for very small charge.'

'How small?' we asked in unison. At this stage we'd already outlaid the best part of (the equivalent of) five Aussie dollars.

His fee worked out at less than a dollar. It all appeared a pretty good risk, and it was, for while we took in the local culture and geography that afternoon he proceeded to cook just about the best seafood feast I have ever had. Whenever I tuck into a seafood meal anywhere in the world, no matter how good the chef might be, he or she will always have trouble beating our little mate from Twaka.

From Twaka, we returned to the Old England club, then to Tanzania and then to Zimbabwe for the final leg of our tour. This was the fourth time I'd been to Zimbabwe, but the first time not connected with cricket. However, inevitably we stayed with friends I had met through the cricket tours. The highlight of our time there for me (though not, perhaps, for Debbie) was a three-day fishing trip up the Zambezi River. This was a boys-only trip away I was told, and I was extremely grateful when Deb said: 'Okay, you go, I'll stay here and look after the pot.'

I was fortunate in that, because 'Old Pat' Paterson, the father of our host Grant, was a regular on the river, we were able to go further upstream than would otherwise have been the case. Consequently, I saw a part of Zimbabwe that few get a chance to see via the river.

The tiger fish we caught (as well as the bludgers that got away) were amazing. They were only little blokes — though I did see some pretty big guys mounted on the walls of a Harare pub — but they had an extremely vicious smile and they didn't like being snared. The way to catch them is to throw a line carrying a spinner — that's a fishing lure, not a Shane Warne or Greg Matthews — into the river and then reel it straight back in. If one took the bait, you had a nice little adrenalin rush on your hands. At one point, I was playing the game while we made a pitstop on the river bank — casting it out and then bringing it straight back in — but I couldn't get them to bite. 'You'll have to get it out a little further,' I was told, so I took a few more paces into the river and then threw the line out there again. Still nothing. I knew they were out there somewhere, so I kept wading in that little bit more . . . until I was waist deep in water. Sure enough, they started biting, and I began to have the time of my life.

Then, from further up the Zambezi, came a speedboat. The bloke behind the wheel slowed to a crawl, doffed his cap towards the shore and yelled out: 'Eh, Pat, how are you? Fishing for tiger?'

'Aye, mate,' Grant's old man shouted back. 'There's plenty here.'

'That's good, mate. But be careful. Freddie's just round the corner.'

'Freddie?' I wondered. 'Who the bloody hell is Freddie?'

'Freddie', I was calmly told, was Freddie the Crocodile. Calmly, but with Carl Lewis speed, I moved back to water a little bit less than ankle deep. While this meant I wasn't going to catch too many tiger fish, I knew it was the right strategic move. Soon after, I gave up and went for a stroll up the river's edge and saw not just Freddie but a few of his mates as well.

The crocodiles were just one species of the abundant wildlife I saw on the banks of the Zambezi. There were elephants and kudus, and hippos who liked to park themselves in the river on just the line the speedboats wanted to take.

By the time we'd completed our adventure, and I was able to look back on my time in Africa, I was sure there wasn't a breed of African wildlife I hadn't seen in the flesh at one point or another.

Soon afterwards, the three of us headed home — Debbie,

Mike and Mike's pot. That it had remained in one piece was a miracle. It was big, it was awkward, it was heavy, but when I got it home and stood it up in the corner of our lounge room, I reckoned it was the best looking pot the world had ever seen.

When we moved house in 1991, it was the first thing transported, and I did it myself. There was no way I was going to trust my exquisite Kenyan earthenware to any removalist. Debbie insisted it stay in the hallway of our new home, which I quickly realised wasn't a bad idea, as it meant every single person who walked through our front door had a chance to admire it. So there it stayed until a fateful day in the cricket season of 1992–93 . . .

During that season, my old captain from Fleetwood in the north of England, Harold Wilkinson, came out to Australia and stayed at our place. One night, Harold had a night out on the turps with a few blokes from the Randwick Cricket Club, and arrived home a little late and more than a little fragile.

The next morning, as he reached for the panadol, he quietly said: 'Ah, Michael, last night when I'm comin' in, I tripped on door mat, fell over and head butted some pot you had out there.'

'Not the big one?' I asked nervously.

'Aye, big ugly brown one. I picked up all th'pieces and put 'em in bin for you.'

'All the pieces?'

'Aye . . . eh, Michael, why you cryin'?'

I really loved that pot.

•CHAPTER 26•

Michael Whitney, Unplugged

One of the hardest things about being a cricket commentator is the earpiece — the tiny listening device that is your link with the director of the cricket coverage. Through that earpiece, during a 20-minute stint on air, you might receive vast numbers of instructions from the director, telling you what he'd like you to talk about, what he's about to put on the screen, when we're going to a break, when we're back on air, what replay he's going to show, that the scorecard is coming up, and so on and so on. That earpiece can be difficult, because all the time, while it's telling you what is or should be happening, you're also required to think for yourself. You're the expert, so you're supposed to be adding your in-depth analysis to what's going on out there in the middle.

Sometimes the earpiece can cause all sorts of trouble. One day, during a NSW–South Australia Mercantile Mutual Cup match at the SCG in 1993–94, I was in the Channel Nine box, on air, with Greg Chappell. It was a fairly quiet time during the South Australian innings, one of those relatively dull periods that can occur during a one-day match, and the discussion turned, after a direction from my earpiece, to the subject of polishing the ball. This was okay by me, because I was one of the great ball polishers and would often end a day's play with a red stain on the outside of both trouser legs and another on the traditional inside-leg area, where fast bowlers and helpful fieldsmen have been shining the ball for years.

Greg and I launched into it, explaining why the ball is polished, what the laws of cricket allow you to do, who's permitted to do the shining, and so on. Then Greg pointed out how, as the ball is thrown back from the keeper to the bowler, via second slip, gully, cover, extra cover and mid-off, each player likes to give the ball a bit of a rub. To add to the effect, our friendly director began focusing on different players shining the ball and ended with a close-up of an unidentifiable fieldsman, the monitor showing his body from the chest down, giving the ball a hefty polish.

While that close-up was being beamed out into a million Australian homes, Greg Chappell commented:

'And there he is . . . the bowler's lackey giving the ball a good shine.'

Which was a seemingly harmless remark, except for the fact that just as Greg uttered the word 'lackey' the cameraman moved his focus up slightly, to take in the face of the fieldsman . . . Richard Chee Quee, a very fine player, a good Randwick boy, and the only man of Asian origin to ever play first-class cricket in Australia. Suddenly 'bowler's lackey' took on a whole new meaning.

I looked over at Greg, just in time to see his lower jaw hit the floor. How unlucky was he? At that very moment, we heard a phone ring out the back of the box and assumed it was the first of the viewers' complaints. Somehow we battled through to the end of the over, and the ad break, and then, as the rest of the crew burst into laughter, Greg shouted: 'Of all people, it had to be Richard Chee Quee!!'

I first began commentating with Sydney radio station 2GB in season 1983–84. My first game was a one-dayer at the MCG, and I'll remember it for one infamous line I threw in right at the start. The 2GB sports director was a bloke called Richard Fisk — the idea of a commercial station covering the World Series Cup matches had been his — and he was calling the ball-by-ball stuff when I came in for my debut as a cricket commentator.

'And it's a very warm welcome to the 2GB microphone for the first time . . .' Richard told his many thousands of listeners, 'to injured NSW and Australian fast bowler . . . Mike Whitney.'

'Good afternoon, Richard. Good afternoon, listeners.'

I was extremely nervous. This was something I had never done before, and just at that moment, I was hoping I would never have to do it again.

A ball was bowled, and then Richard fired off a question.

'Well, Mike, you've been out there in big games such as this,' (which wasn't exactly true — at that point of my career I'd played a grand total of two Test matches and one limited-overs international for Australia) 'it must be hard to pick up the ball with such a huge colourful crowd packed in like the one today?'

'Ah . . . yes, Richard,' I began. 'If you look around the ground (remember, we were on radio), you've got all the red hats, and the red eskies, and the red t-shirts, and a lot of other things red. When the ball gets hit up in the air and the crowd becomes the background you're looking into, it can be almost impossible to see the ball.'

'That's all well and good,' Richard shot back, 'but they're using a white ball out there today, Mike!'

Oh yeah!

On air, I laughed it off, but inside I was a broken man. For the rest of my first session in cricket commentating, my remarks were restricted to things such as 'Yes', 'No' and 'Maybe'. For example, Richard would say: 'That was a great delivery, wasn't it, Mike?' And I would reply: 'Yes.'

Eventually I overcame this setback, and by the early 1990s felt fairly comfortable up in the box, whether on TV or radio. However, I was only a part-timer and I acknowledged my place in the scheme of things. This was especially true when I received the occasional call to enter the Channel Nine commentary box. For me, this was akin to my early days walking into first-class cricket dressing rooms, with M. Whitney once again the young punk among seasoned professionals. I felt extremely humble just being there, with legends such as Richie Benaud, Bill Lawry, Ian and Greg Chappell, Tony Greig, Michael Holding and David Gower. To have the opportunity to share a stint with Richie, the absolute doyen of world television cricket commentary, will always be one of the great privileges of my life.

During the 1993 Ashes series I was given the chance to call the last three Tests for Nine. Throughout that series, as he had on previous tours, Richie was commentating for both Nine and the BBC. Inevitably, the Poms' commentary box was on the opposite side of the ground to Nine's, so Richie would finish a

stint with one network and then have to tramp around the ground to his alternate microphone. At The Oval, his journey from the BBC booth to the Nine box culminated with a climb up a long ladder, to a scaffolded perch constructed especially for we colonials.

One day, when he finally joined us, he commented, in his best Billy Birmingham voice: 'Well, there are not too many people here today. It only took me five minutes and 37 seconds to come around, whereas yesterday it took me six minutes and 20 seconds.' I thought to myself: 'Only Richie Benaud would be able to measure the size of a crowd in such a way.' And because he said it in his famous measured tone, it was very funny.

The thing I'm asked most about the Nine commentators is: 'Do Tony Greig and Bill Lawry really hate each other?' The questions come, of course, because every so often the two, one a former Victorian and Australian captain, the other a South African-born former English captain, get on air and argue quite passionately about the different sides of an issue. And they don't mind pointing out just how ridiculous the other's argument, and consequently the other, is. But the truth is that most of these debates are staged. Tony might give Bill a nudge when they're going for a short break, and tell him what their next argument is going to be. Bill will usually have no trouble taking the other side. Tony might say he's going to give Merv Hughes a bagging, Bill the loyal Victorian is not going to cop that, and after the director has said 'back on air . . . five, four, three, two, one, yours Tony,' they'd begin.

'Well, Bill,' sniggers Tony, 'what about that last over from Mervyn Hughes. He couldn't bowl a hoop down a hill.'

'Which is why,' Bill might retort, 'the big Victorian has only taken more than 200 Test wickets for Australia.'

The argument might go on for overs, and then they'll laugh about it later, off air. They really are good mates.

The best thing about commentating is that it is as close as

you can get to the game without actually participating. I was fortunate to be on air, on Channel Nine, for two very significant moments in Test history. One was the final ball of the fourth Test of the 1992–93 Australia–West Indies series, the game the Windies won by a solitary run. The other was the end of the fourth Test of the 1993 Ashes series, at Headingley, when Australia retained the Ashes.

That Test at Headingley ended when their left-arm seamer and number 11 batsman, Mark Ilott, swung at Tim May and skied the ball up in the air towards Allan Border at wide mid-on. Border ran around underneath it, held it, and the Aussies had won the Test and the Ashes. I was able to tell all Australia how it happened and I thought I did a pretty good job, but it couldn't have been good enough because when it came time for the powers that be to produce a video of the

BILL LAWRY IN THE COMMENTARY BOX

moment for posterity, Bill Lawry's voice was dubbed in over mine. Now, I know as well as anyone that Bill can get a lot more excited in the commentary box than I do — that's just our styles — but the fact was Bill wasn't even in the UK when the Test was being played! It all seemed a bit unnecessary to me.

Greg Chappell was my partner for the conclusion to the one-run Adelaide Test. This was a most remarkable match. On Australia Day 1993, Australia, needing 184 to win but facing Curtly Ambrose and company on a difficult wicket, slumped to 7–74. However, with Test debutant Justin Langer playing an innings far superior to many Test-debut hundreds, the home side clawed their way back to 8–144. Then Langer was out for 54. The Windies looked home, but no-one had counted on the courage and skill of Tim May and Craig McDermott and gradually the final Aussie pair worked towards the winning run.

By the time I came on air for the last time in this Test, the crowd in the outer was singing 'Waltzing Matilda'. Everyone in the place, including the commentators, was on edge, while the guys in the Australian dressing room were firmly planted in their chairs, no-one daring to move. Everyone willed Maysie and Billy to get Australia home. In all his time as a Test cricketer, Allan Border had never been part of a series-winning Australian side against the West Indies. This was his last chance.

There was never any plan for Greg and I to be on air for the finale. That was just the way it worked out. I can tell you I was extremely pumped up as I waited to go on. The last wicket had been out in the middle for the best part of an hour already, and I stood right behind Ian Chappell as he spoke into the microphone: 'Australia need 15 runs. The West Indies need one wicket. They've called in Curtly Ambrose. He's got 24 (wickets) for the series. He'd dearly love to make it 25. In the commentary position now . . . Mike Whitney and Greg Chappell.'

Ian jumped up, unplugged his earpiece, I plugged mine in, and we were away. My co-commentator was already seated.

'Thank you, Ian,' said Greg, 'Plenty of tension all around the ground at the Adelaide Oval, and not least of all in the commentary position, eh Michael?'

'You're not wrong, Greg,' I replied, as I got comfortable in my seat. 'I've been nervous all day.'

Ambrose's first ball was to McDermott, and he sliced it uppishly into a gap in the cover field for a single. We were on our way — 14 to win.

'Every run is like a piece of gold, and the Australian supporters enjoy every one of them,' said Greg, as the crowd roared its approval. 'As far as the West Indian supporters are concerned every one of them will be like a sharp knife in the back.'

The Adelaide fans were not just cheering the runs, they were clapping the defensive shots as well. Even the balls that went through to the keeper, Junior Murray, were enthusiastically applauded. The Aussies were on the verge of winning, and the local boy, Tim May, was going to get them home. His off-breaks had already captured 5–9 the day before, as the Windies crashed in their second innings for just 146. On this final afternoon, the West Indies captain, Richie Richardson, put his faith in his two most experienced and best bowlers, Ambrose and Courtney Walsh. By the time Walsh moved in for the opening ball of his next over, it was past 6pm in the eastern states. However, Channel Nine opted to stay with the cricket, which, while a rare move, was one befitting the greatness of the struggle. Only two years earlier, they had switched off at the Adelaide Oval with Mark Waugh just a few runs short of what proved to be a century in his debut Test innings.

Walsh to McDermott, and the first ball was down the leg-side. The second, a slower ball, was glided down to fine leg for a single, and the crowd roared its approval. 'This has been a very handy partnership,' said M. Whitney. Handy!! I probably should have added that Curtly Ambrose was a reasonable fast bowler, the atmosphere was a shade tense and the Adelaide Oval was a fairly attractive cricket ground.

Our director, Brian Morelli, told us through the earpiece that he was going to a shot of the Australian team watching the action from the viewing area that came out from their dressing room. 'Tony Dodemaide (the 12th man) looks like he's chewing his hand away there,' I told the viewers at home. 'Everybody's very nervous.' Allan Border was throwing a ball — his 'worry' ball — from hand to hand; Shane Warne was puffing at a cigarette. Then May grabbed two, backward of square leg, to reduce the target to 11; 10 to tie.

Walsh dropped the ball short, and May went right back on his stumps. 'Waaiitttt!!' came his call through the tiny microphone Nine had placed behind the middle stump. The crowd went back to chanting 'Waltzing Matilda' — perhaps more loudly than before — and I was trying to think whether I'd ever felt more Australian. The final ball was scoreless, and we went to a break as the batsmen met in mid-pitch and the crowd struggled to recall the words to the second verse.

Ambrose's first ball of the next over was harmless, and the second went for a single, to short fine leg. Ten to win. Again Brian Morelli went for the Aussie dressing room.

'It's hard to know what to do in this situation . . . when you're a team member but you've got no part to play,' said Greg. 'You want to sit there and watch what's going on, (but) it's very hard to relax and enjoy it. Some of them will be chewing on their fingernails; others will be holding their breath, keeping their fingers crossed, all sorts of things . . . (Ambrose bowled) . . . Tim May . . . right behind it once again.'

'I'll tell you what — he's played a magnificent innings, win, lose or tie,' I commented. 'He's been there a long time now. One hundred and 18 minutes . . . 91 very nervous balls.'

A short, scoreless ball later, Brian went round the field, and when he reached the worried face of Desmond Haynes at short leg, Greg commented: 'Hasn't had much to do in the field.' Sure enough, two balls later, May popped a ball up to the leg side. It should have been caught, but Haynes was too slow and too deep and, worse still, the ball snuck past for another single. Nine to get and Nine went for a break.

When we returned, Greg started with: 'Nine runs required . . . a couple of good hits from Tim May will put this game very much within the reach of the Australians.' Walsh charged in, and Maysie drove him through extra cover for three. The crowd at this moment sounded more like a football mob deep into the last 20 minutes of a grand final thriller. I think it was at this moment that the locals really began believing the Aussies would win. The crowd waved their Aussies flags as proudly as they could. In the home dressing room, Mark Waugh, between exaggerated bites at his chewing gum, appeared to be smiling, but for the rest the stern looks on the faces reflected the continuing tension.

'Justin Langer can't watch,' said Greg, who was struggling to make himself heard above the din. 'Shane Warne's not sure what to do . . . Allan Border's playing with that cricket ball again.'

Walsh dropped the next ball short, and McDermott, up on his toes, off-glanced it just short of Brian Lara, the solitary slip. You could clearly hear the bowler's desperate cry of 'Catch it!!' through the ground mike. I was as stressed as the players. I knew I was calling something very, very special — one of the greatest of all Test finishes — and I prayed that I didn't make any mistakes. On instruction from the earpiece, I described the ritual that was being played out in the home dressing room — no-one would be allowed to move from their seats. AB was still throwing his ball from hand to hand. Next delivery, Walsh went for the bouncer and McDermott responded with something resembling a hook shot. The ball sailed through to the keeper.

'Top edge would have been handy there,' muttered a very unbiased Greg Chappell.

The fifth ball brought a very optimistic lbw enquiry, which umpire Darrell Hair turned down, and then McDermott had the last ball to third man to keep the strike.

'Nine for 181, five runs required,' said Greg, and we went to the break.

After we came back, Ambrose pitched the second ball of his over up and McDermott spooned a half-hearted drive towards mid-off. Richardson dashed in from extra cover and swallow dived towards the ball, and for a moment it seemed the match was over. But the ball was low and he had failed by a whisker to get his hand under the ball. Every replay, from every angle, showed what a gallant attempt it had been. Each time it seemed he would just get there, but no . . . the ball spilled loose and the battle went on.

Had Richardson a choice of any man in the world to bowl for him in this situation, it would surely have been Ambrose; the great fast bowler tore in once more. Again, McDermott played a dead bat. Every time Brian Morelli ordered a scan around the ground the cameras showed quite clearly the growing despair of the fieldsmen, and the terrible tension being endured by the fans and the Australian players. One image, more than any other, will stay with me — a close-up of Richardson, his face contorted in a sea of anguished furrows, his body language saying to all the world . . .

'What have I done to deserve this?'

Craig McDermott looked as tense as he was, but Maysie might have been batting in the nets. The stand had been going for 80 minutes now. McDermott was 16, May 41 and now McDermott flicked Ambrose out past Haynes towards the square-leg fence. For a moment it looked like three, but Walsh ran around quickly from fine leg, and the batsmen stayed with the two. Three to win.

'One good hit!' explained my co-commentator.

Then something very unlikely happened. The great Curtly Ambrose, going for the yorker, bowled a full toss. However, McDermott, his weight on the back foot, did no more than push it towards mid-on. How Billy would have loved another shot at it, but, even so, for most the predominant emotion was not of an opportunity lost but another Ambrose threat survived, and umpire Len King's shout of 'Over!' was lost in the cheers of the crowd.

Instead of going for another ad break, Nine stayed with the cricket. There was so much for the cameras to show, and I think the men in charge were fearful a great moment in cricket history might slip past while the sponsors were being kept happy. However, the first ball of Walsh's over changed nothing, and then the second brought another unsuccessful lbw appeal. The replay clearly showed the ball was heading down the leg side. 'Spare a thought for the umpires,' I said. 'It's a very, very tough job at any stage of the game . . . I'm sure Darrell Hair's nervous . . . and Len King at square leg.'

Walsh bowled short again, and May spooned it backward of square, again agonisingly away from and beyond the despairing Haynes. My first thought was it might have been two, but as Ambrose raced in from fine leg the batsmen stopped at one. Just a single to tie, two to win. The home fans roared with delight. If ever Test cricket has been more tense and thrilling than this I have never seen it or read of it. Wherever Brian Morelli turned — to the crowd, the fieldsmen, the Aussie dressing room — he caught the cruel but fantastic tension of the moment. A shot aimed at the commentary position would have done the same.

Richardson talked with Walsh. Haynes stood with arms outstretched — everywhere he had stood in close on the leg-side to that point had been wrong. 'Where should I go now?' Third man came up to about fly slip, which seemed ludicrous, not stopping the one but conceding the two if a snicked ball ran past. Meanwhile, Maysie and Billy chatted in mid-pitch. Nothing, it appeared, was going to stop them now. Finally, the West Indians had their field ready, and the batsmen went back to their marks. Walsh came in, bowled, and McDermott swatted the ball away on the leg side . . .

'There it is!' cried Greg Chappell.

But it wasn't. McDermott had hit plenty of the ball, but up high on the bat, and Haynes, hapless until this moment, somehow stumbled in front of what seemed the winning runs. His left hand knocked it down. McDermott, a step into the first of two, sprang back into his crease, while the crowd, jumping off the edges of their seats, had to recall their victory shouts. Spectators' hearts had never throbbed this hard. Australia had been *that* close to winning the series.

The next ball was driven into the covers, for almost a run, but not even Carl Lewis and Linford Christie would have risked a quick single in such circumstances. Again, the crowd screamed in optimism, as the batsmen took two or three hurried paces before shouting 'No!!', and then cut back their shouts as they realised more was still to come. At this moment Brian Morelli cut back to the home dressing room yet again. Little had changed. AB was still playing with his worry ball; little Justin Langer was now sitting with his chin, elbows and hands resting on the ledge that ran along the front of the viewing area.

'Justin Langer . . . he can't sit up straight now,' I said. 'It's been a torrid time for him in his debut Test match . . . He scored a magnificent 50 runs today . . .'

It was strange. Langer had batted for most of the day, yet it seemed an absolute eternity since he had been dismissed. I guess in many ways it was. For the visitors, just two runs away from losing the Frank Worrell Trophy, the May–McDermott alliance must have seemed as if it had been going on for ever. From the Aussies in their dressing room, the camera focused on the West Indies captain. I continued, as Walsh reached the end of his run: 'Richie Richardson surveying the field . . . what can he do to get this last wicket?'

Walsh came in for the last ball of his over. What followed was a scene that has been played over time and time again. It is a replay that is imprinted indelibly in my mind. The ball was short and climbing, and Billy McDermott tried desperately to get his bat and gloves out of harm's way as it flew through to the keeper. But when Junior Murray caught the ball he raised his gloved right arm triumphantly in the air. Walsh continued on his follow through, arms pointing to the heavens, for many seconds not daring to look back at Darrell Hair. When he did glance back, the umpire's finger was in the air. The ball had nicked Craig's bat AND the peak of his helmet as it whistled through. It was a brave decision by the ump . . . and a brilliant one, surely one of the all-time great umpiring moments in cricket history.

When the ball went through, I wasn't sure if the ball had hit anything, and if it had, what it had touched. So when Darrell's hand went up, I was completely stunned. So was Greg. I think we had both been psyching ourselves up to describe the winning hit.

But life goes on. In the commentary box, Greg called it this way:

'Oh!! He tried to avoid it but it's hit the bat. And he's gone!! . . . The Test match has been won by one run!! I can't believe it!'

For a while after that call — it seemed like ages — neither Greg nor I said anything. There was no need, the camera told the story perfectly and we were too shocked and disappointed to comment anyway. Billy looked down at the pitch, up at the umpire . . . and then dragged himself sadly away. Rarely has Test cricket been so brutal.

Through the earpiece came what seemed like a million instructions, mainly to the camera guys. 'Get McDermott!! Replay!! Replay!! Close-up on Walsh!' Meanwhile, the West Indian celebrations were animated to the extreme. Desmond Haynes punched the air like a centre forward at Wembley. Fast man Ian Bishop, his prayers answered, was down on his knees. High fives were everywhere. The camera's pictures of Walsh clearly showed he was having a lot of trouble believing what he had just achieved. The crowd, stunned for a moment, then burst out into loud and prolonged applause, which reached a crescendo when May and McDermott reached the gate. I was having trouble making myself heard, and as Nine wanted to get out of there and go to the nightly news, pretty much all I had time to say was this:

'Well, what an unbelievable game this has been. For the Australians to fight all the way down to needing one run to tie this Test match . . . Craig McDermott has edged a short ball behind . . . and the crowd is giving the Australian batters a very, very good ovation . . . (the earpiece now told me the replay was going to air) . . . McDermott, trying to pull the bat out of the way of that one and gets a nick through to keeper Junior Murray, and the West Indies are jubilant. (Focus on the successful bowler) Courtney Walsh is ecstatic . . . he'll be a hero tonight in the Caribbean, in his home town of Kingston, Jamaica . . . The series is alive! . . . Richie Richardson is no doubt a very, very happy captain. They've won the Test match by one run. What a phenomenal game!'

The cameras were now showing the West Indians hugging each other, as they gradually made their way back to the dressing room. Brian Lara had souvenired a stump, as had Walsh, who was still the focus of much of the celebrations. Out there with them was their coach, the great Rohan Kanhai, who had batted at three in the first tied Test, between Australia and the Windies at the Gabba in 1960–61. Behind us, in the commentary box, was the legendary Richie Benaud, Australia's captain in that epic game. On the last day in Brisbane he had scored a brave 52 when with Alan Davidson he all but rescued a Test match most thought lost.

The tied Test! The mere mention of that phrase conjures up images for cricket fans of sport as thrilling and tense as it can possibly be. Yet, I know it couldn't have been any more dramatic than what happened at the Adelaide Oval on Australia Day, 1993. I'm not saying the Adelaide Test was better. But it was just as good. And I was there, calling the game at the very end.

I reckon that makes me a very lucky man.

•CHAPTER 27•

Out of the Blue

I was working in my office one day, when I received a call from a man by the name of David Flatman. He introduced himself as a producer of TV 'infotainment' shows, and told me of his plans for a show highlighting Australian innovations and inventions. This was all very nice, I thought, and then he produced the punchline.

'We were wondering,' he asked, 'if you'd like to be the presenter of the show?'

To a bloke whose experience in TV was no more than commentating on cricket, doing the occasional interview and the odd commercial, this was an offer right out of the blue. The advice I subsequently received from people whose opinions mattered to me was that, if I wanted to pursue a career in the media, it was an extraordinary opportunity. And the thing I liked the most was that the show was not directly related in any way to sport. A lot of sportsmen retire, then head straight into the commentary box to describe the sport they've just left. As a result they get pigeon-holed in that role and I didn't want that to happen to me.

David came around to see me the day after we'd first spoken

on the phone to outline the concept and to explain that the first episode, to be co-produced by his production company and ABC-TV, needed to be completed within the next five weeks. That was neither here nor there to me, until David admitted that these sorts of shows usually take more like five months (at least) to get off the ground. The ABC had suddenly announced they wanted the show in a hurry, so off we went — despite the fact that the host of the show had absolutely no experience in, well, hosting shows. For me it was a genuine case of diving in at the very deep end.

The show was originally going to be called 'The Innovators', but it was decided that was more than a little too close to 'The Inventors', the title of a very successful and well-known ABC-TV show of years gone by. So an alternative name — 'Great Ideas' — won the day.

Making the show was a helluva lot of fun. I had a really, really great time. I worked with a lot of very professional people, met some remarkably clever, creative people and learned an amazing amount about television.

The innovation I remember most fondly from 'Great Ideas' was the '30-second' tent, a creation of a fella named Joe Viglione. You know those terrible days when you're camping in the Serengeti Plains in Africa, a massive thunderstorm is looming, the hyenas are on the prowl and you have to get your three-man tent up in a hurry. Right then, Joe's your man; through his ingenious design you can have a spacious little home for the night erect and sturdy within half a minute.

We filmed the 30-second tent segment on a rainy day out the back of David's half acre property at Seaforth in northern Sydney. I remember it was raining because, while we were waiting to begin, I mentioned to Joe that his tent had better work because I didn't want to get wet any longer than we had to. He laughed, and then went about his job. While I stood close to the camera explaining to the viewers what the concept was all about, Joe was in the background breaking the world record for tent construction. In the end he took closer to 20 seconds than 30.

And do you know the most incredible thing about Joe Viglione's tent? He invented it in his dreams. Fair dinkum! One night he grabbed for the pyjamas, put his head on a pillow, fell asleep, and a few hours later the great idea of the 30-second tent was born.

'You mean you dreamt the tent?' I asked.

'Yeah, I dreamt the tent,' he shot straight back. 'I've dreamt a whole lot of things. The tent is just the best of them.'

Joe wasn't the only genius we profiled. There was a guy who invented a mount that made linking your caravan or trailer to your car a whole lot easier. Another person had devised a remarkable water filtration system that could make the ugliest glass of water drinkable. One fellow who'd done some work with worms was a big hit. After years of research, he had developed a product called . . . wait for it . . . the 'doggy-doo-doo disposer', which did exactly what you'd expect it to do. When you're out walking your favourite canine, you take your doggy-doo-doo disposer with you, clean up after your pet's done its business, then whack the contents of the disposer in your worm farm — the worms love it; they develop into big, athletic worms — you then put the worms in your garden (we all know how good worms are for your garden), your plants and vege-tables grow like crazy and you become the talking point of your street and suburb. As simple as that, and all because of all the world's poop, worms love doggy-doo-doo the *most*.

The show was about current ideas, and innovations that had been devised by Australians over the decades. There were such things as the life savers' surf reel, the idea for which researchers believe came from either a cotton reel or a fishing rod reel. Then there was the machine you see on tollgates around the world that can automatically collect your money and let you through without having to say howdy to the toll collector. And refrigerated truck transport, which was created to solve the problems created by the tyranny of distance in Australia.

One of my favourites was a young bloke named Simon Cunningham, who, for the sake of the segment, we called 'Wildlife Boy'. Simon was studying zoology and veterinary science at university, and at the same time working part-time at the Taronga Park Zoo in Sydney. Most importantly, Simon was concerned with the fact that people were poisoning possums which had taken up occupancy in the roofs of their houses, despite the fact it was illegal to kill possums (which are protected as native fauna) in this way. Wildlife Boy decided he would come to the rescue, by offering to trap the possums that were living in the roofs. Having done that, he was available to block up all the possible entry points into the roofs, and to build possum boxes in backyard trees. When Simon told me that there were nearly as many possums as there were roofs in the northern suburbs of Sydney, I realised he was in a position to make a tidy profit. Not that that was his aim — he was more concerned with giving the local wildlife the chance to co-exist with humans in the urban environment.

And the Great Ideas kept coming. Did you know an Australian microsurgeon, Dr Earl Owen, developed many of the instruments used today in microsurgery? Then, when his back started to ache during operations that sometimes stretched over several hours, he invented a chair from which he could still perform the surgery. And from that he designed a chair, now used by many Australian cinemas and theatres, that is a million miles more comfortable and better for you than the old park-benches our parents used to sit on to watch John Wayne's latest western.

Another thing I'll never forget about Dr Owen was an offer he made after we'd finished filming his segment. 'Mike,' he whispered, 'if you ever need a vasectomy, come and see me. I'm one of the few people in Australia who have perfected a cut that's reversible if you change your mind about it later.'

Thanks, but no thanks, doc!

Another great idea involved a design for the rims of road trucks' tyres — called 'Truck Trims' — which meant that, when the truck was being driven on a wet road, the spray was diverted under the truck, rather than being sprayed out into the vision of following vehicles. This has two benefits — one which anyone who's ever been caught behind a truck on a moist highway will immediately recognise; the other being that the truck's brake system, gear box and so on is being kept that little bit cooler as well.

I have a special affinity with truckies. My father was a truckie, and I can recall as a kid being up there in the driver's compartment, sitting proudly by his side, as he drove through Sydney's streets. This is why I was so keen to get involved in a campaign for the Road Transport Forum designed to boost the image of truck transport and truck drivers. From my own childhood experiences, I know truckies are good blokes, I know they do a bloody terrific job, and I know they make a lot of sacrifices to earn the money to support their families.

The fella whose truck we used for the demonstration of Truck Trims on 'Great Ideas' was a bloke called 'Clarkey'. Now he was good value was Clarkey, and I'll tell you a story about him that sums up the character of a lot of truckies. When he pulled up in his truck, our director's eyes lit up. Clarkey's vehicle was covered in dirt, and in no place was it less clean than around the tyres and the tyre rims. The director liked the dirty truck — he called it 'realism' — but Clarkey would have none of it.

'There's no bloody way you're filming my truck dirty,' he explained, before setting off to find a hose, a rag and a chamois. Maybe the ensuing spot didn't look quite as authentic as it would have with a bit of mud on the tyres, but Clarkey's truck looked a million dollars.

A few months later, I was down in Portland, Victoria, which is located just about on the South Australian border, to do a

193

promotion for the road transport forum when a truckie came over to say g'day.

'Howyagoin', Whits?' he called out.

Unfortunately, I was caught in one of those terrible situations we all hate getting in to. I just couldn't place the face.

'What 'ave I gotta do? Lay down in front of you before you'll talk to me?'

Then I had it.

'Clarkey!! The truck trims! Whatta you doin' here?'

'This is where I live . . . in Portland.'

And then he explained how he'd driven from Portland to Sydney for that demonstration for 'Great Ideas' . . . to help out a mate, the guy who'd invented the truck trims. That to me was absolutely amazing.

The public's reaction to the show was great. Our ratings weren't in '60 Minutes' territory but for the ABC they were excellent. We went to air at 8pm on Thursday — immediately after the current affairs show, 'The 7.30 Report', and before the clever political satire, 'The Damnation of Harvey McHugh'. A few weeks after 'Great Ideas' had finished, I was talking to Bob Carr, then the leader of the Opposition in NSW politics, and he told me he reckoned every politician throughout Australia watched our show. Why? Because they all had to watch 'The 7.30 Report' to keep up with things . . . and they had to tune into 'Harvey' to see who that show was taking the mickey out of. I just hope we gave all the pollies an entertaining half hour.

Whatever happens in my future television career, I will always be in debt to the show and the people that produced it. Not only did I have a great time working on the program, I learned a great deal and had the chance to work with very clever, skilful operators. I found talking to the camera a very disconcerting experience at first. It wasn't easy to relax and be myself. After all, there was just me, the camera, a camera operator I hardly knew, a sound man I hardly knew and a director I hardly knew.

In the end I found a little sticker, wrote the name 'Mardo' on it and whacked it on the top of the camera, just above the lens. Mardo is Wayne Martin, my best mate since schooldays, and until I had the hang of things I imagined I was talking to him.

Occasionally during the first couple of episodes I'd look at the scripts I was about to memorise and say: 'Hang on, this isn't Mike Whitney. The Mike Whitney I know wouldn't say it that way.' Fortunately the producers gave me a lot of leeway, and the chance to Whitneyise things a little. After that, things became a bit more relaxed for me and, by the final episode, my presentation was a lot more polished than during my debut performance.

While 'Great Ideas' was my first big break into mainstream TV, it was not my first or last foray into general (rather than strictly sports) television. I've done the odd guest spot, on shows like 'Denton' and 'Live and Sweaty', and appeared in advertisements for products such as 'the all new *Australasian Post*' and Tooheys. Now I'm full-time with the Seven Network, and loving every minute of it. But probably the craziest thing I ever did was to accept an invitation to appear on the 'D-Generation's Late Show' on ABC-TV. My role was to sing the Mike Whitney version of the Whitney Houston hit 'I Will Always Love You', the song from the movie *The Bodyguard*.

The D-Gen's Rob Sitch, one of the funniest and cleverest blokes on Aussie TV, contacted me to explain the 'Late Show's' concept of 'musical mix-ups'. The plan was something like this: Mick Molloy, another of the brilliant talents on the show, was cast as having the job of finding an act to close each show. So you'd have a situation where Mick would be on camera ready to introduce his latest signing.

Another of the cast, usually Tony Martin (no relation to Wayne), would say something like: 'And to close the show this week, we have, performing her latest hit single . . . Whitney Houston!'

And Mick would come back with: 'Whitney Houston? . . .

MIKE WHITNEY GOING OUT TO BAT IN
THE WEST INDIES

I thought . . . I thought . . . I thought you said you wanted Mike Whitney.'

And then I'd come on and try my best. Which sadly wasn't that flash, especially the high notes.

Before I flew to Melbourne for my big performance, the guys from the show sent me up a video of Whitney Houston in action and a copy of the lyrics. And I practised and practised. I really didn't want to make a fool of myself. When the big day came, I arrived to find they'd set up a stage something like that in the actual film clip, and that they had a singing coach there to help me along. So I punched out the tune, and my tutor said I was brilliant. It wasn't until later that I learned she lied.

For the clip, I wore a black jacket, black t-shirt and blue jeans and belted out the tune while a camera man swung around me just like another camera person must have done for Whitney Houston when she belted out the tune in the States. The only difference was that she was paid a fraction more.

After I'd finished, and everyone seemed happy, Rob came up and said: 'Thanks Mike, that was brilliant.' And then he added, 'Ah, Michael, just . . . umm, one more thing . . .'

'Yeah, Rob, what?'

He had a bag in his hand. In it, I quickly found out, was a gleaming silver tiara and a glistening (fake) diamond-studded top.

'In the Whitney Houston clip,' Rob was speaking very quietly, 'it ends with Whitney wearing gear something like this.'

'Yeah, that's not a problem,' I said.

'You mean you'll wear it?'

'For you guys, anything.'

So I did. It was a big finish, and it set off the entire thing (almost) perfectly.

I wasn't the only person to fill this role. After me, David Boon had a shot at David Byrne from Talking Heads, Max Walker did a terrible Cyndi Lauper's 'Girls Just Want To Have Fun', Hayley Lewis was Huey Lewis, Ron Barassi was Shirley

Bassey (fair dinkum!!), 'Baby' John Burgess from 'Wheel of Fortune' had a go at the Baby Animals. They even had the former Victorian premier, Joan Kirner, doing her best impression of Joan Jett singing 'I Love Rock'n'Roll'. We were all bizarre, but it worked.

And the craziest thing was that, I was told later, they didn't receive one knock-back from the people they asked to do the guest singing spot.

Another of my most memorable performances was a guest role in 'Neighbours', which lasted just a single episode. Originally Greg Matthews was cast in the role, but he had to pull out and M. Whitney received a late call-up. It was England '81 all over again. I played the part of Mike Whitney, cricket coach, who had been called in to help the Ramsey Street indoor cricket outfit.

About 12 months after my 'Neighbours' performance went to air in Australia, I received a phone call from the north of England, from Harold Wilkinson, who is perhaps best known in Australia as the bastard who in 1992 smashed the beautiful pot I'd brought back with such care from Kenya in 1987.

'Fookin' hell,' was the first thing he said. 'The lads down the Mount (the Mount pub, which is where we used to drink in Fleetwood) were laughin' last week. Couldn't believe it. Fookin' Whit on fookin' "Neighbours"!!!'

I guess I shouldn't have been surprised. Apparently, each episode of the show is watched by something like 50 million people across the world.

Something seen by a few less than 50 million people were a series of TV commercials I did for the Bottlemart liquor chain. Unfortunately, the punchline to these ads was 'hey, who bottlemarted?', which was a bit of a come down after 'How do ya feel?' But the product was good, the money okay, and the ads, which ran during the 1994 Friday night rugby league matches, were very successful. I just wish they could have come up with a catch-phrase that was a little bit more upmarket. It can be a little bit disconcerting when you're walking down a busy city street, dressed in your best double-breasted suit, in the company of a couple of very senior business executives, and someone yells from across the other side of the street: 'Hey Whit, who bottlemarted?!?'

Such is the price of fame.

•CHAPTER 28•

Dear Jill . . .

Late in 1983 I received a letter in the mail from a lady I had better not name. For the sake of this story I'll call her 'Jill'.

Jill was still at school, in Year 11 I think, and the letter involved a questionnaire that asked things such as what was my favourite movie, favourite food, favourite restaurant, most embarrassing moment, which person would I most like to meet, will you come with me to my formal, and so on and so on.

I tried to answer all Jill's questions as honestly as possible, but I had to decline that last enquiry, which I think explained the real motive behind all the questions that preceded it. I just wonder how many questionnaires from female fans someone like Shane Warne has to fill out these days!! However, despite the knock-back, I kept a copy of Jill's questions and my answers, and looking back at it now, I can see through my answers just how in some ways I have changed a great deal, whereas in others I am still very much the same.

For example, whereas back then my favourite food was Greek, now my taste buds lean more towards cuisine with an Asian flavour. Maybe that's because we have a Vietnamese nanny helping us with our triplets! And I must eat a bit more nowadays, because I weigh 10 kilos more in 1995 than I did

201

in 1983. Back then I drank mainly beer and mineral water, but now I drink more fruit juice, predominantly apple juice. In the old days I collected coins, now I collect cricket memorabilia. Robert De Niro is still my favourite actor, and *The Deer Hunter* my favourite movie, but whereas in 1983 my favourite music was 'Australian bands, especially the Oils and INXS, and Judie Tzuke', 12 years on I'd have to include a few more — Led Zeppelin, Cold Chisel, Paul Kelly and The Doors. And maybe Judie might get relegated back to the reserves.

Jill wanted to know what I considered the 'best thing about fame'. My reply in 1983 was: 'The people you meet and the places you go (not that I'm famous yet).' If I was asked that question now I'd write something very similar, but I'd add: 'The opportunities to do things and receive things you'd otherwise not have the chance to enjoy.'

The worst thing about fame in 1983 was 'the telephone'. It's still right up there, although I am fully aware that many of the wonderful things that have happened to me have started with a simple phone call. However, there are just those times when I wish it would ring that little bit less, and that little bit later in the morning.

According to Jill's questionnaire, my heroes 12 years ago were the champion Australian cricketer, Doug Walters, the champion pre World War I American athlete, Jim Thorpe and . . . Captain Scarlet. Fair dinkum!! Walters, Thorpe and Scarlet. In many ways the choice of Captain Scarlet reflected my youth and the times — I'd bought a Captain Scarlet t-shirt at a street market in London while I was there for the sixth Ashes Test of 1981. When I returned home later in the year everyone was asking me 'Where did you get that t-shirt?' as if it was the greatest piece of gear ever created. 'I bought it in London,' I'd proudly say, with just the right level of arrogance that said you peasants can't get them here in Oz. Every time I put that Captain Scarlet t-shirt on I felt that little bit special. Cartoon superheroes on t-shirts hadn't been discovered at that point in

Australia's history. They have been now. And, you know, I still have that Captain Scarlet t-shirt today. I use it to polish my car.

Dougie Walters is still a figure very much admired by Michael Whitney. In fact, he remains a cult figure not just for me but for just about every male of my generation who ever followed the cricket. Other sporting people I look upon with a kind of awe include Jack Nicklaus, Greg Norman, Shelley Taylor-Smith and Kieren Perkins, while Mark Richards, the champion surfer, is also right up there. I received a huge buzz out of meeting Mark for the first time in 1994, because I consider him to be the best there's been at something I always wanted to be good at. But, even though I admire these stars greatly, as I get older I don't look at people in heroic terms quite so much. I know now they are just flesh and blood like the rest of us. The people I revere the most now are those special people who have stuck with their principles no matter what has happened to them. The present Dalai Lama, the spiritual ruler of Tibet, is one such man. Nelson Mandela is another.

I told Jill my most embarrassing moment came when I was a fourth-grade bowler with Randwick. One weekend, while grade cricket was on a one week's break for Christmas, I travelled up to the Gold Coast for a holiday with my mates from the Mascot rugby league team. While I was there, I happened to run into an extremely attractive lady whose charms were sufficient to keep me up north for an extra week, which meant I left the cricket team a man down. As anyone who's ever played cricket at any level can tell you, there are few worse sins than to leave your team short, for whatever reason, without so much as an apologetic phone call. When I finally returned I was obliged to front the cricket club committee who, after hearing my rather unique (and ridiculous) alibi, opted to suspend me for two games. I was genuinely remorseful . . . and as embarrassed as I ever will be in my life . . . but at least I took heed of the warning and became a much more dedicated cricketer from the moment I walked out of the committee room.

Jill asked me if I had a fantasy I wanted to live out. Twelve years ago I wanted to be a rock star. I used to sing into the shower nozzle, or in the car. Still do. But today I wouldn't swap that lifestyle for the one I have — no way — even though the thought of being a rock star does appeal from time to time. I like the idea of being in charge in front of a huge, screaming mob, where anything you do, no matter how unlikely or inappropriate, is deemed to be creative.

One night in the Snowy Mountains, I had the opportunity to belt out a couple of numbers in front of an appreciative audience. I was there with the NSW cricket team, doing a promotion for Tooheys in a bar at Perisher, after we'd played a game in the snow on an aluminium wicket at Mt Blue Cow. There was a three-man band playing, and suddenly they told the full house that the Blues were in the pub — an announcement that was promptly followed by an invitation to the team to come on stage and sing a song. Moey Matthews suggested we try the old classic, 'Wild Thing', so I jumped up, expecting all of my comrades to join me. It wasn't until I was actually up on the stage that I realised that not one of my beloved team-mates had left the bar.

'Go on Roy!!' they were yelling from the safety of the shadows. 'You'll be right.'

What could I do? I gave a hopeless smile to the 'fans' cheering below me, turned to the guys in the band, and said: 'Okay boys, let's do it.'

And off we went. By the time I was finished I had the crowd in my hands and a couple of women not long past their 40th birthdays up on stage with me. We were having the time of our lives.

Something similar happened on a NSW Cricketer of the Year cruise a few years later, when I was conned in to doing a very ordinary version of 'Johnny Be Good'. Fortunately, the audience were right into the spirit of things, so I stayed on stage and joined in a duet of the Cold Chisel classic, 'Khe Sanh', with a very eager Michael Slater. Each time, it was a real buzz to see the people in the bar reacting to what I was trying to do on stage. To do that sort of thing in front of tens of thousands of people, in an enormous stadium, and knowing you're good at what you do, must be an awesome adrenalin rush.

In 1983 I told Jill my 'best' cricket match was the previous season's Sheffield Shield final, when NSW travelled to Perth and defeated Western Australia. Even today, with my career now over, that game ranks very, very highly on my list of great games. But for pure emotion and pride, the one I'd put top of the list from my life in cricket would be Australia's astonishing come-from-behind victory in the first Test of the series in Sri Lanka in 1992. I don't think that win has ever really received the acclaim in Australia it merited. We were 291 runs behind on the first innings, yet we won the Test, with Warney taking 3–0 in 11 balls right at the end to seal a stunning 16-run victory.

From a purely personal point of view, my best two games of cricket were the two Test 'seven-fors', against the Windies in 1989 and India in 1992. The 7–89 in Adelaide was great, because I finally silenced the critics, while the 7–27 in Perth three years later was just a golden day. I couldn't have bowled any better.

When I think of my best days in cricket, a couple of Mike Whitney batting exploits spring to mind as well. I remember one last-wicket stand I shared with Dutchy Holland, when we put on 70 against Western Australia in late 1982, in a game we eventually won outright. And another partnership, with Murray Bennett just two weeks later, when we added 45 for the 10th wicket to gain a first-innings victory over South Australia at the Adelaide Oval.

After that Adelaide triumph, NSWCA Secretary Bob Radford told Rick Allen of the now defunct Sydney *Sun*: 'It was the best Mike has batted since the Tooheys television advertisement'.

Funnily enough, the bloke I belted through the covers in that commercial (which had been filmed 12 months earlier), the great Joel Garner, was bowling for South Australia. When I went out to bat, my colleagues had been less than optimistic, but I turned and said: 'Don't worry fellas, she'll be right.' And she was. I finished with 10, including a four — only the second first-class boundary of my career. 'The first one was in the Tests against England last year, when I edged Ian Botham for four,' I explained at the time. 'This was the first time I've hit one off the middle of the bat.'

It was a cover drive off John Inverarity. Absolutely awesome!!

When Jill asked what was my 'worst' cricket match I replied: 'Never played one.' And I never did. Some, obviously, were better than others, but I never played a real shocker. There were always a lot of other, less interesting things I could have been doing.

'What do I do when I'm not working?' was the second last question Jill fired at me (as I explained, the final one was about that formal I never made it to). In 1983 it was 'relaxing'; in 1995 there's much less time for that, because I'm working so much, and because I have three very special children to give my time to. If one thing sums up the way my life has changed, it is the lack of 'spare' time I now have. But I'm not complaining — I love my family, my work, my life just the way it is at the moment. I still try to get to the beach for a few minutes when I get the chance, and if we can get someone to look after our triplets, Debbie and I appreciate the chance to visit a good restaurant.

These rare quiet moments are extremely precious. The demands of parenthood, especially in our case with three babies joining the family all at once, have been extremely difficult. My life has been turned upside down in a way I could never have expected in 1983. But, you know, despite all the stresses that revolution has brought, I wouldn't change a thing.

•CHAPTER 29•

The Masters

In early March 1995 I had the opportunity to be a part of an Australian team that travelled to India to compete in the inaugural World Masters Cricket Cup. This was a tournament staged by the Cricket Club of India. It was played exclusively in Bombay, and featured a smorgasbord of outstanding veteran players from six countries — Australia, England, India, South Africa, Sri Lanka and the West Indies.

The full Australian squad was Geoff Lawson (captain), Terry Alderman, Murray Bennett, Greg Dyer, John Dyson, Kim Hughes, Bruce Laird, Wayne Phillips, Jeff Thomson, Mike Whitney, Graeme Wood, Graham Yallop and Bruce Yardley. Not a bad side at all. Among our opponents were a selection of cricket greats — men such as Gavaskar, Garner, Gatting, Rice, Dujon, Viswanath, Le Roux, Venkat, Randall, Gomes, Van Der Bijl, Snow, Greenidge, Barry Richards, Viv Richards, Vengsarkar, Graeme Pollock, Kallicharran, Underwood, Kapil Dev, Croft. Not surprisingly, the event turned into a competition that more than caught the imagination of the public.

Because of a personal commitment, I wasn't on the same plane that took the rest of the team as far as Singapore, on the first part of their journey to the sub-continent. But the lads had a 10-hour stopover there, and I was only eight hours behind, so when I landed at Singapore's international airport I was able to catch up. The first blokes I ran into were Woody, Flipper and Roo Yardley, and they were quick to tell me of a remarkable effort put in by one of our team-mates on the flight over. He had celebrated the fact that he was back touring with the boys again by making a brave attempt at emptying the plane's liquor cabinet.

His display, from all reports, was . . . what can I say . . . extremely loud and, especially in its final moments, more than a little unattractive. Flipper couldn't decide if the performance was appalling or outstanding. Roo remarked that if the player's form on the plane was any indication, he was heading for a highly interesting tournament. Woody just shook his head. Soon afterwards, I ran into Henry. The first thing I said was: 'G'day, Hen, how was the flight?'

'Not too bad,' he replied, 'but you should have seen . . .'

I told him not to worry about it.

Then I saw John Dyson. He was swift to mention our colleague's extraordinary effort, but then he related another tale, which reminded me that we were a team of EX-international cricketers. Back in Sydney, Dyso had just finished packing his bags and was about to leave for the airport when the phone rang. It was Murray Bennett's wife, Jane.

'John,' she yelled through the phone, 'I'm glad you haven't left. You must come over here on the way to the airport.'

'Why?'

'Because,' she said in a very anguished tone, 'Murray's forgotten his body.'

A million different thoughts ran through Dyso's brain. He had to give this scenario quite a bit of thought. 'What,' he finally asked, 'are you talking about?'

'His two knee guards, stomach support, ankle guards, hamstring warmers, elbow guards. He put them all in a big bag, checked them just before he left, added an extra couple of jars of Dencorub, but now he's left the bag behind. The poor dear won't last a net session without them!'

So Dyso travelled to the airport via the Bennetts' place. And then he had to haggle with a customs guy over the amount of excess baggage costs he was obliged to pay.

From Singapore we flew to the heat of Madras for a two-hour stopover, and then to the chaos of Bombay, to begin our preparations for the Masters.

One of the first places we visited was the Cricket Club of India. The club is based in a magnificent building that backs onto the Brabourne Stadium, the main cricket ground of Bombay. Both the club itself and the premises it calls home are extraordinary examples of the great wealth and opulence that exist in this country. The foyer is all marble, with 10-metre ceilings and exquisite works of art peering down from every wall. I was told it costs the equivalent of a mere 150,000 US dollars to join the club, and then 7000 US dollars a year to be a member. And they have 7000 members and a 30-year waiting list!

In the days leading up to our first game we practised at Brabourne, taking advantage of some superb facilities. The practice wickets were outstanding, and we all ran in pretty hard — except Thommo, who in the main concentrated on his leg spin.

However, there was one occasion when Thommo did bend his back in the nets. The team's liaison officer was a young committee member of the Cricket Club of India called Sachin Bajar, who I had met during the previous Australian season when I guested for a NSW Cricket Association team. Sachin was in Australia at that time, played with me in that game, and after finding out that I would be a part of the Australian Masters team had put his hand up to be the chaperone for the Oz team in India. It was an outstanding move from our point of view, because he never failed us once. Everything he promised came true.

Sachin was keen to have a bat in the nets against the legendary Thommo. This was something, he informed us, he would be able to tell his grandchildren about. But Thommo was not too keen — he reckoned if he bowled flat out he'd 'make an Indian rug out of him'. But our little friend was insistent. So Thommo sent down a few, and nearly killed the poor fella.

While we practised, back in the Members' Pavilion, some of the local gentry were playing cards on these fabulous, antique tables which were located in a long, glorious room between the two dressing rooms. Later in the day, after the practice sessions were completed and as the sun headed for the horizon, many of these card schools were transferred outside, onto the lawn where a plethora of cane tables and chairs had been brought out. Upstairs was another magnificently decorated area — the reading room — where distinguished gentlemen turned the pages of the day's *Bombay Times*, and every so often lifted their eyes to see what might be happening out on the playing field (perhaps their new champion, Sachin Tendulkar, might be making an appearance?), or to acknowledge the waiter who had left another Scotch and ice on the nearby table.

This was opulence of the grandest order. But it was hard to come completely to terms with. Still fresh in my mind was the memory of the abject poverty that is a fact of the streets of Bombay, and especially the great slum (supposedly the largest in the world) that crowds the road that runs from the airport to the city centre.

In all, we were in India for 13 days. Unlucky 13. Seven of those days had been declared 'dry' by the government — that's 'dry' as in you can't drink any alcohol. There were elections scheduled, and the pollies wanted the electorate sober when the votes were cast and counted. The fact that we weren't voters didn't get us an exemption, which meant we had to employ some pretty politically unacceptable means if we wanted a drink.

One night, we went to a reception at a very classy restaurant but because of this drinks ban the waiters were offering nothing stronger than Diet Coke. However, there was grog about. More than one Master had smuggled in his own supply. In fact, one South African brought so much in that when he asked me to hold onto his jacket for a second I nearly dislocated my shoulder.

One of our blokes managed to get a few cartons of Heineken past the security guards (he'd shrewdly wrapped them in brown paper), which led to a funny situation. Basically, it was a case of the old have-a-swig-from-the-can-and-then-hide-it-back-under-the-table trick. And then place the can, when empty, behind the marble column near the table. Everything was going fine, but then a waiter noticed a pile of about half a dozen empties. He walked over, picked up one of the offending items, shook his head, scooped up the rest of the cans and walked away.

Half an hour later he was back, to play out the same charade. He looked genuinely bewildered as to how they could possibly have got there. It reminded me of that time in Sri Lanka when Warney had no idea how a pile of dirt kept reappearing on his bed. The waiter kept cleaning up the cans, time and again. By about his fifth visit, I had to say something. 'Hey, matey,' I said, 'what's going on?'

'Heineken,' he said, pointing to the three or four cans near the column, 'arriving from nowhere.'

Then he picked up the empty cans, and shuffled slowly away. What he didn't know couldn't hurt him.

The next day, while most of us slept in to lunchtime, Roo Yardley was up and about. He hailed a cab and asked to be taken to the Kaleela Markets.

'I'm after a new watchband,' Roo explained to the cabbie, as he jumped into the front passenger seat. 'A bloke I know told me that was the place to go.'

'Oh no, sir,' said the cab driver, 'you should be going to Victoria Markets, not Kaleela. I will take you there.'

CLIVE LLOYD

'No, mate, my mail's pretty good,' said Roo. 'I think I'll stick with Kaleela Markets.'

'Oh no. No, no, no,' the cabbie was adamant. 'Definitely you should try Victoria.'

'Kaleela's fine.'

'No, no. Victoria, definitely. Without doubt, sir.'

'Look mate,' Roo was getting pretty angry now. 'I want to go to the fucking Kaleela markets. If you don't want to take me, I'll get out and find another cab.'

'Okay, sir, no problem,' the cabbie muttered, like a young child conceding that Mum was right yet again. Although he did whisper once more: 'But you should definitely be going to Victoria.'

So they set off to Kaleela Markets. But when they arrived there wasn't another soul in sight.

'See, sir,' announced the cabbie triumphantly. 'All closed!'

Roo never did get that watchband.

On the night following Roo's misfortune, I sat down for dinner with, among others, the great Clive Lloyd, a wonderful statesman of the game who was not playing but had been given the honour of being named Tournament Chairman. During the evening, he related a stack of stories. My favourite concerned a situation in Adelaide some years before.

The West Indies team of that time had a favourite nightspot or two in the city, and one night Clive arranged to meet the rest of the lads. But when he arrived none of his comrades were there. No problem — he just ordered a drink and propped himself at the bar.

Clive hadn't been there long, when a good looking young lady walked up and introduced herself.

'You're Clive Lloyd, the West Indies cricket captain, aren't you?' she asked.

'That's right,' said Clive.

'Ah, I hope you don't mind me asking,' the girl continued. 'But what shoe size are you?'

'Um, er, I'm a size 12, why do you ask?'

'Well, ah, it's just that my boyfriend is stuck outside because they won't let him in wearing runners. He's a big man like you, and I thought you might be the same shoe size. In fact, he's a size 12, too.'

'And you just thought I might lend you my shoes so he could get in?'

'Yes please . . . if you don't mind?'

Clive wasn't silly. He figured that as soon as he gave her his shoes, she'd be out of the place and he'd be minus shoes.

'I'm sorry,' he said, 'but there's no way I'm going to fall for that one.'

'No, no, no,' she cried, 'I'm telling the truth. Here, I tell you what . . . I'll leave my handbag here. There's more than a 100 dollars in it, and my driver's licence. We'll be straight back.'

Clive thought for a moment, looked at her pleading face, and realised she was almost certainly fair dinkum. So he bent down, ripped off his lace-ups, took her handbag, and went back to his drink, confident that in a few moments his size 12s would be returned.

But then he paused, looked around, and realised he was the only person in that bar who was black, barefooted, and carrying a handbag. Every single person in the place was staring right at him. No matter how quickly that bloody girl came back, it wasn't going to be quick enough!

One concern Clive and his fellow Masters organisers had was that the players wouldn't be sufficiently serious. But they had no need to be worried. From the jump, every cricketer on every team was chasing the win and the contests were competitive and extremely well received by the public. At a pre-tournament function, I spoke to Gary Davey, the Chief Executive at Star-TV, the Asian-based cable network that was covering the matches. Why, I asked, did they want to broadcast this type of cricket? Because, Gary replied, there were something like 50 million satellite dishes in India alone. As almost every person in India loves cricket, that still means there are a lot of ardent followers of the game with access to cable television. In all, Star-TV gains exposure in 53 countries throughout Asia. With those sorts of stats, it wasn't difficult to find companies who wanted to advertise their products between overs. For 10 consecutive days, matches were televised live in their entirety.

The prizemoney was substantial — 50,000 pounds to the winning side (West Indies), 20,000 pounds to the runners-up (India), and 500 quid to each man of the match.

Unfortunately, we lost both our matches, to the Windies and England, and consequently failed to make the semi-finals. In our first match, the legends from the Caribbean belted us for 311 off their designated 45 overs. Jeffrey Dujon and Gus Logie hit big scores, while Viv Richards hit Henry for a collection of his trademark sixes. In reply, we managed 257.

Following the game some controversy arose over Gus Logie's involvement. Not long after he had been presented with the man-of-the-match award, a local journalist pointed out that he was 34 years and six months old, which was six months less than the stipulated age. Then someone else pointed out that while the rules and conditions stated that you had to be retired from first-class cricket, more than half the English team were still playing county cricket and Mike Gatting had scored a Test century only six weeks earlier! In the end it was decided to ignore these transgressions, but they did leave a bit of a sour taste. One thing we all believed was that next time (and after the success of the inaugural Masters there's going to be a next time), the people making the rules should tighten these sorts of things up.

Against England we lost by 15 runs, but at least I bowled okay, taking 3–35 from my nine overs. A buzz for me after this game came when a number of genuine greats of the game came up and congratulated me on my performance. People like the South Africans, Vincent Van Der Bijl and Barry Richards, made a point of saying I had bowled well.

Away from the cricket, the local culture was always intriguing and often bizarre. With me always was that blatant chasm between rich and poor. The rich were very, very wealthy, yet poverty was apparent just about everywhere. And the saddest part about the plight of India's poor is that they really have nowhere to go; no opportunity to inspire their lives. They have nothing. And yet they accept their way of life, stay as cheerful as they can, and survive from day to day.

Now that I'm back home, I look at our land of Oz only in terms of good. There's no bad — it begins at good and climbs to fabulous, brilliant and fantastic. I don't think there's anything bad about Australia.

John Dyson was obsessed by the local taxis, which went by the brand name of 'Padmini'. Dyso discovered there were different versions of the Padmini — the Premiere, the Deluxe and the GT. The Premiere Padmini has its gearstick on the steering column; the Deluxe has the gearstick on the floor; and so does the GT. But what makes the GT so special is that it also has mudguards complete with a chequered-flag design. That's the only difference, but only the most exclusive of Bombay taxi drivers get to drive the GTs.

Dyso's other obsession on the tour was his good health. He had heard all about touring cricketers catching the Bombay Bug or the Delhi Belly and it wasn't going to happen to him. The only runs he wanted were the ones he scored in the middle. Every precaution was taken, every potentially bodgy meal was ignored, even to the point where he left the sensational local ice cream untried. But it was all worth it, because when John Dyson jumped on the flight to take him back to Singapore (via Delhi) he had not even had to put up with a headache after a night on the sherbet. And he was more than a little proud of this fact.

'It's just a pity,' he grinned at me as we looked for our seats on the plane, 'that some of the other guys haven't got the iron-hard constitution of Johnny Dyson.'

Dyso was still chuckling as we tucked into our meal during the first leg of our journey. But not long after we climbed out of Delhi's airport, that grin departed, as his face slowly turned into a ghastly shade of snow white. And then he made his first short sharp sprint for the toilet, knocking hosties and stewards out of his way as he dived for safety. The airline food had got him. For the rest of the journey, from Delhi to Singapore, then Singapore to Brisbane, and finally Brisbane to Sydney, we hardly saw him. But then he emerged, not long before we began our final descent. He looked terrible although on the mend, and even managed to keep up with us as we walked towards our loved ones who were waiting at the Arrivals gate. In fact, he made it to about five metres from his wife, but then the bug grabbed him one last time, and after a quick peck on the check and an anguished 'good to see you, babe' greeting, he dashed away again.

But good as Dyso's performance was, it isn't my favourite memory of the first World Masters Cricket Cup. One of the funniest (although I'm not sure if Dyson would agree with me), but not my favourite. To me the idea and beauty of the whole tournament was summed up by one solitary delivery. Srisnivasaraghavan Venkataraghavan — 'Venkat' — the famous Indian offie and now a respected Test umpire, bowled to the great Graeme Pollock of South Africa, who turned a ball to short fine leg where it was fielded by India's revered captain, Sunil Gavaskar. Three legends, dare I say it, three Masters of the game, back in front of a big crowd doing their thing. It was a small, but golden, moment.

To have been able to share the experience of the first World Masters with such champions, and to participate in the action, is a memory of my later cricket life that I will always treasure.

•CHAPTER 30•

Parenthood

In June 1994, Debbie and I became parents for the first, second and third times. All at once!! We had triplets, who go by the names of Fergus, Madeliene and Juliette Whitney. We knew well before the birth that all three were coming, but although we realised our lives were going to be turned upside down we had little concept of just *how* dramatic and *how* rewarding that turnaround would be.

For the first 10 years Debbie and I spent together, we were freelance in the way we went about our lives. We were a team — a team of two. If we felt like going out, getting away, doing whatever, we did it. At our own pace and in our own time. However, caring for three fragile little babies at the one time is too big a workload for one person. It's just not possible. Now, for Debbie and I to go out at the same time, there must be TWO people at our home to look out for the kids. Of course, this means we have just about lost that freedom that characterised our lives for so long. But I wouldn't change a thing. What we have gained has been so much more.

Inevitably, the change in our lifestyle has led to more than the odd triplets joke. Such as the time, not long after their births, when a good mate of mine rang to offer his congratulations. He was clearly impressed, and labelled me 'the only bowler to ever get a hat-trick with two balls'.

Not long after, at a function where I was the guest speaker, I ran into this same bloke. While I was giving my presentation, I started talking about the triplets and said: 'A lot of people wouldn't know, because it was never made public, but we were on the IVF program . . .'

Whenever I bring the subject of IVF up, what immediately follows is a hush, because many people see the subject of IVF as being somewhat taboo. A lot of people don't like talking about it, as if it hints there is something inadequate in you. But it's just a fact of life that not everybody is compatible with everyone else in every single way. I've met a lot of very classy, very caring couples, who are on the IVF program and are desperate, absolutely desperate to have children. The fact that they can't is extremely cruel.

While most people were working out exactly how they should respond to my revelation, my mate couldn't resist. He was on his feet, hand in the air. 'Mike, Mike,' he was yelling out. 'Mike, does this mean that you are the only bowler in history to get a hat-trick on a deck that wasn't doing anything?'

Some would say that was in bad taste. I'm one of them.

I remember one of my relatives ringing to congratulate me not long after the triplets' births. Discussion went on for a while, until I explained that the kids had been born 'through IVF'. After that, there was a long pause.

'Oh, I see. Ah . . . are they as good as HCF?'

Then there was Dean Jones, who sent me an invitation to play in his tribute game in late November 1994, six months after the kids were born. The invitation was all nicely typed out, and finished with an extravagant 'Dean Jones' autograph. Then, handwritten, was a brief message which read:

'Triplets? Does that mean you did it three times in one night?'

Only Deano would have written that.

One night, while Debbie and the babies were still in hospital,

Parenthood

I went out for dinner with Greg Matthews and his wife, Gillian. At one point, Greg asked when the triplets were coming home. 'About two weeks,' I replied. He then grinned, leaned over the table, gave my shoulder a rap, and said: 'Big Roy, get ready for the ride of your life!'

Greg, as usual, was SOOOOOOO right!

I had always wanted to have children. I saw it as some sort of completion of a circle that began when I came into the world. As you get older, and you see your friends and family with children and you see the pleasure those kids give their parents, you slowly come to terms with the fact that you want to experience that joy as well. It's not that you want it solely because everyone else is doing it. It's so much more than that. For me, having kids of my own, being responsible for them and helping them through the world, appealed as a magical and rewarding thing to do.

Debbie and I tried for quite a while to start a family, and the fact that we were struggling was a source of much disappointment. The thought began to gnaw away — perhaps we were fated never to have kids — but I coped, as I have with other setbacks, because of a philosophy on life I have always held. If things out of your control happen or don't happen, they happen or don't happen, and there is nothing you can do about it. I looked at the consequences of our frustrated ambitions, and appreciated that there were other things — travel, a more extravagant lifestyle, etc — that we could have that would have compensated in some part for not being able to start our own family. I've seen the world and know only too well that you can count on less than one hand the number of people who have everything in life.

Fortunately, the IVF program came to our aid, and provided me with the biggest challenge of my life. Raising the triplets — especially during the first six months — has been the hardest thing I have ever confronted. And yet, compared to what Debbie

221

has been through, I have had it so easy. What I've had to go through has been a cakewalk compared to the stress and turmoil she has battled through. Bringing up newly-born triplets is bloody hard work, and for the mother *relentlessly* hard work. For just about every hour of every day, Deb has to be there to care for all the needs and problems these three little people have.

As I have said, the upheaval in our lives was dramatic and far reaching. Everywhere I go now, people talk first of the triplets and then of cricket, something I would have thought quite bizarre before they were born. But now it is quite logical. After all, they are more important. While I remain an avid fan of cricket, more than anything else I am a father to my children and a support for my wife. Great a game as cricket is, it is still only a game, whereas my children are the world to me.

Yet I look at my kids and cannot believe that I actually contributed to creating them. The way the human race evolves as it does is a source of much wonder to me and to think I am now a part of this cycle. My children are a part of me, and, with Debbie, I am responsible for them, responsible for their upbringing, their education . . . much of their lives. I will be there for them until I die. If they ever have a problem — emotionally, financially, physically, whatever — they will, hopefully, be looking to their parents for support, and I will be making sure I am always there for them.

That, of course, is a big responsibility, but the prospect is something I look forward to. There is nothing wrong with being responsible for wonderful things.

When we take them for a walk, every passer-by stops. 'Aren't they cute,' they all say — which, of course, they are, but I'll reply: 'Not at three o'clock in the morning when they're all on fire.'

At other times, people have asked me, in the best-meaning way possible: 'Don't you wish you had had just had one?' My answer is simple. As a parent, I have never known it any other way. And they're such good-looking little kids; I wouldn't change a thing. But it has been so hard, and there is so little information out there to help us out. Raising triplets has been an exciting, but arduous and difficult adventure. I have suggested to Debbie, quite seriously, that she write a book about her experiences at some point to fill what is a very real vacuum in publishing. Books already written on raising kids might devote a chapter to twins, but nothing on triplets. I guess you're supposed to read the twins chapter twice. The truth is that raising triplets is 10 times as difficult as raising twins, simply because the human body only has two arms and two arms into three babies doesn't go. Raising quads would be harder still.

To bring up triplets, the mother must have help ALL the time. We have been lucky because, as we are relatively comfortably off, we can afford to bring in some paid support. And we have a truckload of friends who have been super helpful.

However, not everyone is that lucky. The fact that any government support is strictly means tested means that raising triplets can put financial stresses on a family way beyond the imagination of most people. We are pretty lucky but I know many other people who are not so fortunate.

I look at what Debbie has gone through, and my admiration for her courage and resilience is enormous. I also look at my own mother now in a different light. 'You went through all that for me?' I ask her from time to time as we discuss the challenges of raising newly-born children. I'm not sure I would have the patience or the endurance to put up with what my wife has been through, both before and after the kids arrived.

Her reward is the amazing experience of watching Fergus, Madeliene and Juliette grow. They were so small when they first arrived. Juliette, the youngest and tiniest, was so little I could put my fingertips under her chin and cover her entire body with the palm of my hand. She weighed 1.2kg. Yet, as fragile as she and her brother and sister were, they were not seen as being in any grave danger in the hours after they were born. Sure, they had to be watched closely, but there were other kids riding a much skinnier tight-rope than ours. I will never forget the panic of one mother in the same ward, who suddenly realised one of her twins had forgotten to keep breathing. Simple, and as potentially tragic, as that. The poor little bloke had been born many weeks premature and his survival instincts hadn't been built in just yet. Thankfully the medical staff had things back in working order in time, but the incident made me realise, once again, how lucky we were and how much attention and care my fledgling new family was going to need.

My three kids spent the first two months of their lives in hospital, in the King George V in Sydney, and never for one moment of that time was I less than in total awe of the care, dedication and skill the staff there gave them. They are truly remarkable people. Just recently, I was asked to speak at a fund-raiser for the hospital, on the theme of 'Caring For You and Your Family'. So, instead of Viv Richards and Merv Hughes stories, I was up there outlining my ideals as a family man and describing the stresses of raising three new-born children under the one roof. It seemed a long, long way from that day in Adelaide in late 1981, when I made my faltering speech to the Cricket Society gathering about my brief experiences as a Test cricketer in England.

I am so proud of my family. I looked at the three babies early in their lives, and tried to work out what was going through their little brains and whether they had any appreciation of the environment they had entered. I wondered how much they understood, and what they saw. I know they quickly recognised Debbie and me — our smell, our presence and our voices, or at least the tone of our voices — and came to appreciate we were on their side. Even today, more than a year after their birth, it is fantastic to watch their bodies develop and to see them gradually understand bit by bit the things we adults take for granted.

I believe they have changed my approach to my career and improved my work ethic. The attitude I now have, and have had ever since I knew they were coming, is that I have to get out to work, to give my children the very best opportunity possible. No more lazy days. My parents gave me every chance, and I want to give my kids the same. I think how competitive the world is today — if they are going to be successful then they are going to need a big start. This was reinforced by an article I read soon after they were born which stated that the amount of information available to the world doubles every two and a half years. That is a quite staggering statistic. The same writer suggested that today's HSC students have already absorbed more information on average than their grandparents did in a lifetime. As I read through that essay, I thought about my children, about what they are going to learn and see in their lifetime, and what resources they are going to need to live successful lives. Things aren't easy — it's a very fast and complicated world we live in.

As early as the first summer after he was born, I had Fergus, on my knee, watching the cricket. I have absolutely no ambitions for Fergus to be a Test cricketer — if he grows up and enjoys the game, that'll be great — and I assume he had absolutely no concept of what was being played out in front of him on the big screen. But I still told him: 'That was a Steve Waugh cover drive, that was a Shane Warne flipper, that was an advertisement between overs . . .'

You never know, it might help. If he grows up to gain as much pleasure from sport as I have done, he'll be a lucky boy.

Fergus, Madeliene and Juliette have brought so much affection into our lives. The thing I appreciate most about them is the loving atmosphere in which Debbie and I now live — so many people, friends, family, everyone, genuinely care about both our own and our children's welfare. Anyone who comes to our home seems suddenly to forget the stresses of the world and become cheerful and chirpy. It's as if no-one is game to be angry in front of the kids.

And I must admit, I'm the same. You just can't help but smile when they're around.

At the age of twenty-one — having played only seven first-class matches — a left-arm fast bowler debuted for Australia. Mike Whitney's first-class cricket career was to be a roller-coaster ride, highlighted by some brilliant bowling performances and soured by a long list of injuries and omissions from test sides.

After his testimonial year in 1992–93, injury finally ended his thirteen year, first-class career in February, 1994. This coincided with the launch of his phenomenally successful autobiography *Quick Whit*.

Mike is currently involved in many projects. He works at Channel Seven, hosting both 'The Weekend Report' and 'Sydney Weekender'. He is the spokesman for the Road Transport Forum, consultant to a computer graphics company, and is a highly sought after motivational speaker with his own promotions and marketing company.

Mike lives in the eastern suburbs of Sydney with his wife Deb and their triplets.